# The World
# Is a Really
# SCARY
# Place

# The World Is a Really SCARY Place

## CONFESSIONS OF A WORLD-CLASS PHOBIC

Roger Lefkon

ISBN: 978-1481183116

Printed in the United States of America

First Edition

*For the three most important women in my life:*
*Phyllis, my soul mate and best friend,*
*Susan, my fabulous daughter,*
*and Gabby, my adoring Yorkie—*
*all of whom have somehow managed to survive my phobic behavior*
*and go on to lead normal lives*

# Contents

## Introduction

The dictionary defines *phobia* as a persistent, irrational fear that can interfere with the ability to socialize, work, or go about everyday life.

While just about everyone is afraid of something, I am afraid of *everything*. Without playing favorites, let me tell you that my list of anxieties includes a fear of heights, germs, dentists, new technology, reunions, earthquakes, choosing where to be buried, growing old, and a prolonged erection. I am even afraid of ugly people; in medical parlance, I have cacophobia, the fear of ugliness. My phobias began to surface the moment I was born. After months of confinement in a safe haven, I was suddenly and reluctantly thrust out into the open space of the delivery room. I panicked and was immediately diagnosed by the obstetrics staff as suffering from agoraphobia, a fear of open and public spaces. To my chagrin, going back was not an option.

And so it went over the years, as I succumbed to one phobia after another. Phobics, like hurricanes, come in different categories. I would unquestionably qualify as a category five and consequently think of myself as a world-class phobic, whose myriad fears embrace many of life's daily experiences. Sadly, I continue to obsess about most everything—especially things that are never going to happen.

I have written this book not from a medical or scientific point of view but rather as a collection of comedic confessional essays. As you read on, you will undoubtedly begin to identify with some of my favorite phobias. This experience may not cure what ails you, but I do hope it will entertain you, and it should certainly make you feel better knowing that you are not me.

Onward—unless of course you have a fear of turning the page. . . .

# 1.

# Everyone Is Afraid of Something

*It's true: everyone is afraid of something. By this point, you might be afraid of reading this book. But what makes truly dedicated phobics such as me special is that we are afraid of many things. Or maybe most things. Or anything and everything, really. Here are just a few of my top fears.*

## Fear of the Unknown

My first encounter with fear of the unknown occurred prior to my formal entry into the world. The initial eight months of my stay on earth were a relatively pleasant experience, with a hospitable living space that enabled me to float in a luxurious spa-like environment, lots of snooze time, and, best of all, round-the-clock womb service with a strict no-tipping policy. It wasn't until the thirty-days-and-counting warning light appeared on my smart phone that I began to develop a fear of the uncharted territory that existed outside my upscale neighborhood. It was not unlike being incarcerated for fifty years, just getting used to the routine and perks that come with seniority, and then unexpectedly receiving a Get Out of Jail Free card. I was overcome with doubt and apprehension about what awaited me on the outside.

When the moment of truth finally arrived, I was still unprepared. However, since going back was not an option, I readied myself to be delivered by an unknown obstetrician surrounded by an unknown medical team, to have my vitals recorded by an unknown member of the Department of Weights and Measures, and then to be hand- and footprinted—although I thought that it was a bit premature for me to be enshrined on the Hollywood Walk of Fame.

Undergoing exploratory surgery is another experience that brings with it a foreboding sense of the unknown. What will they find? Rusting surgical instruments from a previous operation resting comfortably in my abdomen? A pouch of illicit drugs planted by a revenge-seeking nurse who I refused to have sex with? A doctor's misplaced college ring? A titanium joint from a robotic arm? Or perhaps a contact lens belonging to a hospital resident who sneezed while sewing me up?

Before my marriage, going out on a blind date was always been one of my most feared encounters. I spent many hours agonizing over the best place to get acquainted. Obviously, it should be a quiet setting. That restriction immediately ruled out a Wayne Newton concert, but it brought into play skydiving, a silent movie, or maybe even a car wash, if my date and I remained in the car. Yet I always wound up settling on dinner at a romantic hideaway, such as my mother's house.

Every step of this uncharted territory was fraught with danger and uncertainty. What if my date were ugly, what if she thought I was ugly, what if my phone started to vibrate, what if we ran out of things to talk about? And if we were not hitting it off, would I get

11

stuck with the entire bill or just the menu items that I had ordered? Blind dates were truly an abyss of the unknown that could only be topped by venturing into the uncertain world of speed dating, where I did not fare well at all. During my allotted five minutes I always seemed to ask the wrong questions: Have you ever been arrested for a crime? Would you enjoy meeting my parakeet? His name is also Roger, so you may have difficulty in telling us apart. If you had three wishes, would having my child be one of them? How do you feel about cannibalism? And the one that usually ends the session: Do you keep kosher?

The unknown ingredients in some of my favorite foods are also a cause for concern: the beige-colored substance that is found in the dumplings drifting in my wonton soup; the eclectic mix of animal parts that lies beneath the casing of my favorite hot dog; the alluring slabs of edibles that appear on sticks at outdoor food stalls in such places as North Korea, Somalia, and Guinea; the suspicious morsels of meat that are dropped into a shabu-shabu pot, which I like to describe as potluck; and then there is the mixed grill served, family style, at the Katz's diner in downtown Xian. History tells us that the terracotta warriors gathered here for a final meal before heading into battle. Those who skipped Katz's survived to fight another day, while those who ate there perished. To quote my aunt Bertha, who never ever seemed to get it right, "Better that it should make you sick than that you don't eat at all."

There are many unknowns that plague me. Among them are the suspicious airline passenger who sits alone quietly fiddling with his prayer beads; the toy that resides at the bottom of a Cracker Jack box (will it be a highly prized decoder ring or a worthless bird whistle?); the card that is lying face down in front of the blackjack dealer (what will the next one out of the shoe be?); a letter bearing the return address of the Internal Revenue Service; the mysterious flutter in my chest (is it simply gas or something more serious?);

and the quest to discover new sexual positions, the kind that do not require an on-call orthopedic surgeon.

Perhaps my greatest fear of the unknown is what awaits me on the other side of death. Will angels be sent down to transport me to Heaven or will I have to find my own means of transportation? Upon my arrival will I be able to sit on soft clouds, sip jasmine tranquility tea, and consume Wolfgang Puck hors d'oeuvres while chitchatting with old friends and relatives, or will I have to pass an entrance exam before being permitted to pass through the Pearly Gates? If the latter, will everyone I owe money to be lined up to collect, or will I have done the smart thing and listened to my accountant, applied for a reverse mortgage, and then declared bankruptcy before the fatal day arrived? If I pass muster, will I have unlimited visitation rights to earth and thus be able to sit courtside next to Jack Nicholson and Angelina Jolie at Lakers home games? Will all of my doctors who told me to give up smoking, drinking, and eating spicy Chinese food be waiting to tell me "We told you so"? Where will I go to find an all-white wardrobe—does Carroll & Co. maintain a branch in Heaven? Will I have to abandon the credo that has defined my life, "The best thing about kids is making them"? What if after looking over my resumé, God says, "Because you lack goodness, purity, and selflessness, you cannot stay here," and then places me in the *Paradise Lost* high-speed elevator, equipped with Muzak playing fifties standards, and presses the down button? That would be a hell of a way to end my day, wouldn't it?

### Fear of New Experiences

When it comes to filling a prescription I always agonize over whether I should experiment with a generic drug, which is cheaper and whose name is generally more difficult to pronounce, or stay with the more costly name brand, which, in my judgment, is safer

13

and thus less of a threat to my chances of ever collecting Social
Security. Even though I have been told repeatedly that there is little
or no difference between the two, I always opt to go with the more
expensive name brand. I am convinced that generic drugs cost
less because they use inferior ingredients and are manufactured
in contaminated laboratories utilizing the questionable skills of
medical school dropouts, pharmacists who have lost their licenses
in malpractice suits, and drug company reps who have failed to
make their sales quotas. So why change, when in my heart I know
which brand will always come out on top in a blind tasting?

Although my car owner's manual clearly states that
regular gasoline is all that is required, I fear that my engine will
underperform if it is not fed a steady diet of more expensive high-
octane fuel. This decision not to change, saving a few bucks in
the process, is based on several considerations. Premium gasoline
clearly attracts a more upscale and affluent class of people who,
because they are healthier and wealthier, are less likely to leave
dangerous, highly contagious bacteria on the pump handle. It
is a proven fact that many users of regular gasoline go straight
to the emergency room before ever reaching the safety of their
garages. Then there is the matter of odor. If you are like me and
you regularly disregard the warning not to top off your tank, you
will inevitably incur some tank overflow, and this spillage will, in
all probability, wind up on your hands, trousers, or shoes. Now,
should this happen, it is important to recognize that high-test
gasoline smells a lot better than regular, and thus it can more easily
be passed off as a hot new fragrance and help immeasurably in
attracting single woman out walking their dogs. This is important,
because as a rule service stations are not the ideal place to pick
up girls. Also, when your fellow motorists see you reach for the
pricey stuff, they will immediately identify you as a class act, a
captain of industry, and someone to be trusted in a crisis. Because

of these admiring looks, you will feel better about yourself, your self-esteem will rise, and you will sleep better at night and require fewer trips to the bathroom.

Another fear of mine is becoming dependent on Viagra, Cialis, or Levitra. While the men and women in the TV commercials appear to be getting it on in convincing fashion, the fact remains that an erection that lasts longer than four hours can definitely interfere with postsex activities, such as sleeping, urinating, and accessing emails. An out-of-control heartbeat, stuffed-up nose, profuse sweating, and a panic call to my doctor would be a high price to pay for longer-lasting sex, which is why I have always subscribed to the station-break–length theory of sex, which leaves me more time to have a late-night snack and debrief my partner.

High up on my list of new experiences to avoid are certain forms of sex. As an avid reader of *Playboy*, I have often marveled at the myriad positions that are available to sexual partners but have always resisted straying too far from the safety and comfort of the missionary position, even though its apparent religious significance has always been lost on me. I believe it was Sigmund Freud who once said that the man should always be on top in order to avoid personal injury to his ribs, kidneys, and scrotum.

I've always wanted to experiment with a vibrator, but I'm not mechanically inclined. One evening I decided to give it a go, only to have the battery case open at the moment of climax, spewing AAA batteries in places where they were never intended to be. When the lights went, on my partner discovered to her dismay that one of the batteries was missing. To this day it has never been found, although she now sports a mysterious and rather captivating yellowish glow. Like the box step, the missionary position, for all its simplicity, is here to stay.

I have always been fascinated with the prospect of engaging in group sex. As a matter of fact, I have a piece of artwork displayed over my bed depicting a ménage à trois. The only problem is that the third person is a dog not unlike Gabby, my Yorkshire terrier, who, after being forcefully removed from the center of my bed, always manages to reappear at the most inopportune moments, licking everyone and everything in sight. Basically, my concern about group sex is the composition and motivation of the rest of the group. Let's say that there were eight of us. Who would I partner up with initially? Would the sorting-out process be based on looks, religion, age, affinity for ethnic food, sanitary habits, political affiliation, and/or TV-viewing preferences, and would this information be available to just me or the entire group on a need-to-know basis? Would I be better off with complete strangers, people I already know, or a mix of the two? And, in time, would the complete strangers become dedicated, lifelong friends from whom I could get stock tips and borrow money? Furthermore, I would insist that everyone submit to a thorough physical exam as a condition to participation. Who knows what blood tests, MRIs, and dental records might reveal? While I am reluctant to allow myself the experience of group sex, I am nevertheless intrigued by the fact that when it was over we could all go out for Chinese food together.

Although eating is one of my favorite experiences in life I have always been fearful of trying new foods and tend to remain loyal to the things I grew up with. No amount of money could get me to try duck, venison, veal, fish (the exception being gefilte fish) or the three deadly *L*'s: liver, lamb, and loin. I survive solely on a diet of chicken, steak, hamburgers, and pasta.

My one concession to experimenting with something new came early in my relationship with a person who has turned out to be a lifelong partner, although the revelations in this book could change all that. We were away for a romantic weekend and she encouraged me to try a favorite of hers, lobster. After several Beefeater martinis I finally acquiesced and let the waiter fit me with a large bib while I anxiously awaited the arrival of a black lobster that had suddenly turned red. Driven by my lust for this woman, I very tentatively approached the denizen of the deep after first assuring myself that there was no pulse, and then proceeded to devour the entire lobster, ignoring the stringy stuff that was caught between my teeth, and drowning the meat in a garlic butter sauce while at the same time consuming large amounts of white wine to steady my nerves. After repeated visits to the lavatory to floss my teeth and spray my mouth with Binaca, I pronounced the experience a modest success and looked forward to a night of passionate lovemaking. Regrettably this was not to be, as the lethal combination of gin, wine, garlic butter, and Binaca combined to send me to an early and deep sleep. When I awoke the next morning, I was surprised to discover that I was completely naked but still wearing my lobster bib. I could not remember, and never did find out, just exactly how I had ended up in this state.

When it comes to the supermarket, I have remained loyal to all of the brands I grew up with and although tempted to experiment with new products, I have never gone over to the other side. My loyalty rests with creamy Skippy peanut butter, not Jiff; great-tasting Philadelphia Cream Cheese, not Borden's; rich and flavorful Häagen-Dazs rather than that upstart Ben & Jerry's; seltzer from a seltzer bottle, not Perrier; legendary Hebrew National Beef Franks over Ball Park Franks; Nescafé coffee, not Seattle's Best; Campbell's soup—forget Wolfgang Puck; Heinz ketchup and their other fifty-six brands, rather than Hunts; and Fox's U-Bet chocolate syrup, with Hershey's a distant second. While its conceivable that several of these alternative brands might actually be better, I have not nor would I ever consider defecting.

To do so would be like trading in my dog for one who didn't bark, was not so needy, and did not talk in her sleep.

Another new experience that I have flirted with is the desire to join all of those happy faces cruising along in the carpool lane. I am envious of those lucky people who get to whiz by me as if I am standing still, yet I cannot bring myself to join them. To begin, with it's against the law to enter the sacred lane unless you have a companion in the car with you. I generally drive by myself, though, on occasion I have thought about picking up a homeless person for a couple of hours to accompany me as I transition into the carpool lane. You can generally find them at the entrance to the freeway looking quite fit and displaying a homemade WILL WORK FOR FOOD sign. I also fear that when I'm driving with the big boys I will become terrified that the intimidating center road divider will propel me into a head-on collision, and if I should some how survive and my rental companion doesn't, how would I explain his presence to the authorities? On one occasion, in a moment of weakness I actually did enter the carpool lane. After sixty anxiety-filled seconds I tried to escape, only to discover that the solid white line had made me a virtual prisoner in my own car. With the speed limit reading 65 mph, I was reluctant to go any slower than my already reduced speed of 30 mph for fear that the frustrated, angry, horn-blowing parade of drivers backed up behind me would erupt into road rage and suddenly and without warning transform the relative tranquility of the carpool lane into a lethal combat zone. This confrontation was avoided when up ahead the solid white line magically turned into a life-saving broken line, enabling me to move out of harm's way. Fast lanes are like fast women, not for the faint of heart and better left to the young and restless.

## Everyone is Afraid of Something

### Fear of Getting Lost

My earliest recollection of getting lost is of an incident that took place during a school field trip to the zoo. A female classmate and I became separated from the rest of the class and wandered into the Great Ape House. After many hours we were eventually found there by the zoo patrol, feeding bananas to a family of gorillas, and brought to the lost-and-found department. Finally we were rescued by our teachers' missing person's search-and-rescue team, narrowly escaping a terrible fate: according to zoo policy, lost kids were auctioned off to the highest bidder if not claimed within twenty-four hours. That would have been a harrowing experience, considering that we were both only eight years old at the time and lost in each other's arms. She later went on to become a world-class primate therapist while I carved out a career as a quality control expert for Chiquita.

Since my Roman ancestors were known to misplace their horse-drawn chariots occasionally, it comes as no surprise that I have spent hours roaming parking garages in search of my lost car, occasionally hitching a ride in a security guard's golf cart to aid in the hunt. Note: these carts only accept exact change, and there is no charge for the guard.

Over time I have devised a system for each of my car-parking adventures, so when, for example, I take the grandkids to Disneyland to spend some of the cash they have accumulated in change from using their vast inventory of gift cards, I always head for the Seven Dwarfs section of the parking lot and pull into one of their signature spaces—Grumpy's, if it's available. Is it no wonder then that the Dwarfs section of the lot has become the destination of choice for Smart Cars and their attention-seeking owners, such as me? While this game plan works most of the time, there are occasions when none of the spaces are available. When that happens, and I am forced to park in a less memorable spot, I must resort to using the panic button on my remote key to locate my auto at the end of the day. Bear in mind that improper use of this device can and will result in setting off a chorus of flashing headlights and honking horns from all of the Smart Cars within range, which leaves me to believe that Smart Cars may not be that smart after all.

As hair-raising experiences go, however, none are more foreboding than getting lost in space, so think twice before booking passage on the Virgin Galactic Space Ship *Enterprise.* You could be propelled past the International Space Station and out into deep space before the warm nuts and first cocktail are served, and there would be no Spock or Captain Kirk in sight to save the day. With signs that read BLACK HOLE STRAIGHT AHEAD, NO U-TURNS, and NEXT EXIT 10 MILLION LIGHT YEARS, you would do well to take along an ample supply of space snacks (Mars Bars, Milky Ways, Starbursts, Astro Pops) and confirm in advance that the *Enterprise* is equipped with Wi-Fi and an extensive library of DVDs, including the entire six seasons of the TV series *Lost.* You might ask, "Why go?" The answer of course would be, "Because of all of those frequent-flier miles."

Getting lost has become a regular occurrence for me. I have no trouble going from point A to point Z, it's all those points in between that I can never find. Driving is at best a dicey situation, since I have no sense of direction, cannot read maps, and have long since given up trying to comprehend the navigation system in my car and the mysterious lady who resides inside it. Furthermore, driving outside my comfort zone always seems to bring me into contact with streets that either have no names or have names that are virtually impossible to find, places such as Sesame Street, Tin Pan Alley, Easy Street, Lovers' Lane, Skid Row, Yellow Brick Road, Penny Lane, and a destination made famous by Ol' Blue Eyes, My Way.

## Everyone is Afraid of Something

I constantly lose my place when reading a novel (I'm okay with comic books) and have also been known to get lost in my dreams, which an out-of-work actor posing as a shrink once attributed to my losing my way in life. To which I say, "Losing my way has always been a way of life for me." I even get lost in my own home, and that's not easy to do, considering the fact that I live in a one-bedroom apartment. But when I do leave home, as a hedge against getting lost, I'm always accompanied by my homing pigeon, aptly named Lost Leader. This breed of pigeon can travel six hundred miles without losing its way, is fun to be with, dines modestly on fruit, grains, and nuts (essential for growing new feathers), and is surprisingly inexpensive to acquire. I paid fifty dollars for mine, but you may be able to do better with a Groupon. Always register your homing pigeon with the NPA (National Pigeon Association). The dues are modest, and they send you a monthly newsletter.

Here is some final food for thought. When you reach a fork in the road and are fearful of making the wrong decision and getting lost, follow the advice of that great philosopher Yogi Berra, who once said, "When you reach a fork in the road, take it."

## Fear of Climbing Mount Everest

It all began as I was listening to the score from *The Sound of Music* and was captivated by the Mother Abbess singing "Climb Every Mountain" to Julie Andrews. Right there and then I made the decision to place climbing a mountain at the top of my bucket list, leapfrogging over becoming a Walmart greeter, organizing my sock drawer, catching a fly in midair and teaching it to do tricks, stealing a horse from Santa Anita and riding it naked down the 405, and getting a vanity license plate to justify my establishing a bucket list, one that read B4UDIE.

The immediate problem confronting me was my lifelong fear of heights, which, among other things, has limited my ability to drive over bridges, act out my Superman fantasy of being able to leap tall buildings in a single bound, throw my ex-wife off the top of Masada and watch her do a triple somersault into the Dead Sea, and walking a tightrope over Niagara Falls during the high season. To illustrate the depth of my neurosis, I should note that I even avoid social climbing.

Having made the decision to climb a mountain, the next question was, which one? There was only one rock worthy of my fantasy, and that of course was Mount Everest. Imagine a transplanted Brooklyn-born Jew placing the City of Beverly Hills flag on top of the world. Surely the *Beverly Hills Courier* would see the wisdom of preempting George Christy's full-page spread and devoting the entire space to an exclusive Q&A with me, complete with eye-popping fashion photos captured on my iPhone at a height of 29,029 feet.

To insure that I survived this adventure, my team would include all of my medical specialists: Lou Fishman, my internist and golf instructor; Bill Chow, my neurologist, in case I landed on my head; P. K. Shah, my cardiologist, to help deal with labored breathing; Wendy Hoffman, my dermatologist, to keep tabs on the condition of my skin and tell amusing stories about her kids; Robert Klapper, my orthopedic surgeon, to mend anything that might require mending; Joe Caprioli, my ophthalmologist, to insure that floaters did not impair my view from the summit; and, for good measure, Tom Sokol, my colorectal doc, to keep things flowing. Talk about an A-team!

With my medical safety net in place I began to focus on who could guarantee that I would survive the notorious Khumba Icefall (where most climbers who die on Everest meet their maker), reach the summit, and then find my way down the mountain without being taken and held hostage by Maoist rebels. Clearly my only chance of ever seeing the inside of Nate 'n Al's again would rest with my selection of Sherpas. I remembered that it was Tenzing Norgay who guided Sir Edmond Hillary on his historic trek to the pinnacle of Everest, and so I approached his descendants in hopes of recruiting a handful of super-Sherpas, and after tough negotiations with William Morris Endeavor I was able to announce to the world that Murray, Manny, and Max Tenzing were on board and would be joined by their sister Mildred, a struggling reality-show producer for Nepal TV.

It was all downhill from here. I purchased my Gortex windsuit, ice ax, Zippo lighter, crampons, goggles, Dr. Scholl's foot powder, rope, oxygen tanks, satellite phone, altimeter, and *Mountain Climbing Manual for Beginners* online using my Tibetan Groupons. Next I turned my attention to food.

I stocked up on Lipton tea, porridge (the good stuff that appealed to the three bears), biscuits, hard salami (Everest is no place for anything soft), Campbell's Chunky Classic Chicken Noodle Soup (with ample pieces of white-meat chicken), nuts, dried fruit, Reese's Pieces, and that old standby, Spam. As a backup, I packed takeout menus from all of Kathmandu's Zagat-rated restaurants.

Trying to be pragmatic, I decided to survey the scene before making a final decision to attempt the climb and flew into Delhi, hopped on to a Buddha Air flight to Kathmandu, and then boarded an Agni Air flight to Lukla, where I rented a large goat to take me to a local monastery for the night. There the monks treated me to a meal of steamed dumplings filled with fresh water buffalo meat, a dining experience befitting a former TV executive. Fortunately I had removed one of the airsickness bags from the plane and was able to put it to good use.

The next day I hailed a taxi to take me to base camp, an expensive proposition when you consider that it's 17,000 feet straight up, and the fare is slightly higher if you opt for a cab with snow tires. But after sitting in front of the fake fireplace and hearing the locals talk about the unrelenting winds, avalanches, unpredictable snow storms, brutal temperatures so cold it feels like venturing into the fresh produce section of Costco, the fatality rate among first-time climbers from Brooklyn, and the absence of cable TV and a reliable dry cleaner, I decided to pack it in and return to the sunny weather that defines Beverly Hills.

While I still enjoy listening to "Climb Every Mountain," I have abandoned any thought of acting out my fantasy of conquering Everest. Currently at the top of my bucket list is going back in time to discover how the pharaohs of Egypt prepared for a colonoscopy.

### Fear of Heights

Webster's dictionary defines *height* as the highest limit, a relatively great distance above a given level. I define *height* as any vertical distance greater than the height of the tallest NBA player.

My fear of heights has become more intolerable as I have grown older. When I approach a suspension bridge—think Verrazano Narrows or Golden Gate—and I glance up at the enormous towers that hold the cables, I immediately begin to panic. This is accompanied by profuse sweating, a racing heartbeat, blurred vision, difficulty breathing, and the fear of imminent death. I pull the car over, move quickly away from the driver's seat, and let someone else take over. If I am alone, I call 911, AAA, a radio talk show . . . whatever it takes. If I am a passenger on a mountain road, I will attempt to reduce my stress level by pretending to read something, anything—a map, a takeout menu, the car owner's manual, the contents of my wallet. These distractions seldom work, and sooner or later I will be drawn to the window, eyeing the flimsy guardrail that could never prevent a child's tricycle, let alone a grown-up eight-cylinder, three-ton steel behemoth, from going over the edge.

When booking a cruise I always insist on a cabin with a balcony, only to find myself later standing in front of the open veranda door too terrified to step outside for fear that I will fall or be blown overboard. My passion for skiing came to an abrupt end when I experienced similar feelings while sitting in a chairlift, imagining myself slipping out from under the safety bar at any moment. Apartments with terraces, unless they are fully enclosed or are on the second floor—better yet, on the ground floor—bring on the same dread. On a recent trip to Disneyland, my grandson asked me to take him on Space Mountain. My response was "Go with your mother and father, and I'll meet you in the gift shop."

Because of my fear of heights I will never know what it's like to look out from the highest point of the Sears Tower in Chicago, stand on top of the great pyramid of Giza, take the elevator to the apex of the Washington Monument, see Paris from the Eiffel Tower, take in the sights from atop the Coney Island Parachute Jump, or ride the 525-foot-high Star of Nanchang Ferris wheel in China, where a full rotation takes an agonizing thirty horror-filled minutes.

My fear of heights has reached such extraordinary proportions that I can no longer bring myself to watch one of my favorite films, Mel Brooks's *High Anxiety*.

## Fear of Elevators

I will climb ten flights of stairs to avoid using an elevator and would never dream of entering one alone or without a bottle of water and a cell phone.

25

I always look to see when the elevator I am about to enter was last inspected and whether the same service person has returned within a year, a reassuring sign but by no means a guarantee of a safe ride.

Personal experience has taught me that those red emergency phones generally do not work, and that if they do, there is seldom anyone at the other end to hear you. The ideal number of elevator mates is three; more than that and you run the risk of running out of air before help arrives. I also look for strong, tall people who are able to access the small escape route in the ceiling of the elevator. If the door does not open within three seconds, it's panic time. There is nothing more frightening in life than having to pry open the doors of an elevator with your own hands and then find yourself starring at a concrete wall.

High-speed elevators in tall office buildings and hotels are the most frightening for me. Once the initial floor designation disappears from the elevator display panel I begin to break out in a cold sweat at not knowing how high up I am. I begin to think about how devastating the crash scene will look on CNN if the cables should snap. But my worst fear of all is being held captive in one of those pill-shaped exterior devices that ride up and down the sides of buildings, providing an unobstructed view of a fatal free fall to the pavement below.

Now that I think about it, the only satisfying experience I have ever had in an elevator was to see the door open and an Otis maintenance man step inside with a state-of-the-art tool belt, a satellite phone, and enough food to help me survive until the door opened again.

### Fear of Confined Spaces

Throughout recorded history there have been many who have found joy in confined spaces. Count Dracula loved to spend his daytime hours reclining in his velvet-lined coffin, waiting to rise as the ultimate creature of the night; Superman used a telephone booth to transition from mild-mannered Clark Kent to the Man of Steel; Ramses II entertained visiting royalty and an occasional female companion in his tomb deep beneath the pyramid bearing his name; Jacques Cousteau explored the ocean depths in his claustrophobic bathyscaphe while munching on Mrs. Paul's Crunchy Fish Sticks; and let's not forget Elisha Otis, who pioneered the development of the cramped lift known as the elevator and along the way experienced many ups and downs.

I on the other hand, am not a kindred spirit. My fear of confined spaces began when I was a kid and visited the Cape Cod Maritime Museum. That night I dreamed I was a passenger on a four-masted schooner that a glass blower had placed inside a bottle and sent floating out to sea. In time I outgrew my confined living quarters, and while being tossed around on the high seas during a violent squall my protective bottle shattered, and like Jonah I was swallowed by a whale and forced to subsist on blubber, dead fish, and partially eaten cheese pies courtesy of Original Ray's Pizza underwater delivery service (their motto: "If your pizza arrives cold and damp, it's on us!"). When I awoke from my dream and looked in the mirror, my face was covered with melted mozzarella.

Then there was the time that I went to retrieve my vacuum cleaner from its resting place, when without warning the door closed, sealing me inside the broom closet. There I was, trapped in a tall, narrow space with a dangling lightbulb, a concrete floor, and no food, water, cell phone service, or dental floss. A place that reeked, with a musty, dusty, damp odor. Taking stock of my situation, I realized that I was surrounded by feather dusters, ironing boards, and brooms of all shapes and sizes: a stiff, strong corn broom ideal for sweeping sidewalks and warding off muggers; a short synthetic lobby broom with three-inch bristles, perfect for picking up body parts; a late-model, long-handled push broom with a flat head designed to push aside disgruntled office employees, and a whisk broom, small and triangular in shape, used to brush clothing and, in rare circumstances, to scramble a couple of eggs. As the hours passed, my calls for help went unanswered and my situation was becoming desperate, when suddenly the door swung open and confronting me was the one broom that had been missing from the closet, that cigar-smoking, beer-guzzling, fifteen-hundred-year-old green-skinned witch with a wart on her nose. Yes, I had come face to face with Broom-Hilda!

Being confined in a soundproof acoustic room about the size of a photo booth (the kind that produces blurred images routinely rejected by passport control) is something that I had to endure after exhibiting symptoms of hearing loss. Telltale signs included turning up the television sound so loud that even my collection of clowns left the room, constantly asking friends to repeat themselves even when they had nothing important to say, and being unable to hear the faucet drip. Once inside the booth, you are isolated from the outside world, although the audiologist is visible through a small viewing window. You put on a headset and record your responses to a sequence of high- and low-pitched squeal-like sounds by pressing the button on a handheld remote device. Failure to adhere to these instructions will only prolong your captivity, so it's best to play along. Alternatively the audio lady may ask you to repeat words and phrases such as *ignominiousness*, *antidisestablishmentarianism*, *electroencephalograph*, *supercalifragilisticexpialidocious*, and—one that I had no difficulty in repeating—*ménage à trois*.

Perhaps my greatest fear of confinement was realized when I was placed in an MRI machine with no room to move, barely enough air to breathe, and a constant knocking sound rattling my brain. To make matters worse, I developed an itch on my nose that quickly spread to the rest of my face, migrated south to my genitals, and eventually settled in at the bottom of my feet. As a torture device for eliciting state secrets, thirty minutes inside an MRI is infinitely more effective then waterboarding, electric shock, or feeding the victim chicken salad that has been left out in the hot sun for three days. This is a diagnostic adventure that is not well tolerated by those among us who are squeamish, spineless, lacking courage, and profoundly timid—in other words, someone just like me.

Over time my fear of confined spaces has been exacerbated by spending time in a snug womb plotting my exit strategy, zipped up in a sleeping bag with a damaged zipper, and stuck in a sauna with the temperature rising. But one of the most memorable such experiences for me occurred while I was attending a concert and got locked in a portable toilet that had reached its sewage-holding capacity. As I reassessed my life in this solitary confinement, it occurred to me that Neil Diamond must have had me in mind when he wrote "Solitary Man."

I have also been packed into a crowded subway car populated with murderers, terrorists, rapists, and mutual-funds salesmen, and I once fell into a vat filled with chocolate and nuts, emerging as a real life Nutcracker Sweet.

My most public display of confinement occurred immediately after I once landed at LAX. The only thing standing between me and the baggage claim was a revolving door. I thought that I would be able to make it through the briskly moving door without waiting for the next revolution, but as I entered, the revolving door slowed to a halt, trapping me within the metal-and-Plexiglas cage. I started yelling and pounding to no avail as my fellow passengers gave me disapproving looks on their way to pick up their luggage. Finally airport security arrived, and seeing a sign that read BREAK GLASS IN CASE OF FIRE, determined that since there was no fire they could return to home base and continue playing fantasy baseball. I began to get dizzy from the constant turning, and I was losing my orientation and feeling helpless, when in desperation I used my cell phone to call my housekeeper, Bianca, who is quite adept at solving mechanical problems. She arrived with a wire coat hanger in hand and in a matter of seconds was able to facilitate my escape, much as she had done for her uncle Francisco when he was a guest of the Costa Rican prison system.

The lesson to be learned is, what goes around comes around, but only if you are very careful.

### Fear of Friday the 13th

Because I suffer from paraskavedekatriaphobia, which sounds like a popular Greek delicacy, but is in reality a fear of Friday the 13th, this day is particularly challenging for me. A good day to remain at home, stay under the covers with the doors locked and fingers crossed and, in the tradition of Harry Houdini, to pull a rabbit out of a hat and rub its foot for good luck. My dread of Friday the 13th started early in life when, to the dismay of my parents, I chose to skip my thirteenth birthday, which fell on a Friday, and just stay twelve for two years.

There is much to fear about Friday the 13th, considered by many the unluckiest day of all, an event even more unlucky than walking under a ladder, breaking a mirror, spilling salt, opening an umbrella indoors (unless of course it's raining indoors) and watching a black cat cross your path—and I'm not talking about Ray Charles, Count Basie, Ella Fitzgerald, or Satchmo. And for all of you history buffs, legend has it that if thirteen people sit down to dinner together, one will die within the year. That's probably why you never see a table set for thirteen on the patio at Spago: the negative PR would have serious consequences for chef Wolfgang "Wolf" Puck's business.

## Everyone is Afraid of Something

The number thirteen has been much maligned and clearly suffers from its position, following the much friendlier number twelve, which boasts twelve months to a year, twelve inches to a foot, twelve eggs to a dozen, and twelve signs of the Zodiac. As to the number thirteen, many hospitals have no room thirteen, tall buildings skip the thirteenth floor, airlines omit gate thirteen, row thirteen, and seat thirteen, and they will not hire flight attendants younger than thirteen unless faced with a particularly tight job market. In Formula One racing there are no number-thirteen cars, there are thirteen steps leading up to the gallows, and who can forget that Brooklyn Dodgers pitcher Ralph Branca was wearing number thirteen when he served up the home run to Bobby Thompson that was heard "round the world"?

On the other hand, there are some positive aspects to the number thirteen. We began our history with thirteen states, the Apollo 13 astronauts defied the odds and made it safely back to Earth, Michael Jordon wore a size thirteen sneaker, and Mary-Kate and Ashley, better known as the Olsen twins, appeared together in public for the first time on Friday the 13th—the day that they were born.

Friday's bad reputation goes all the way back to the Garden of Eden, where on a Friday Eve tempted Adam with the forbidden fruit. Adam bit and as we all know they were both ejected from Paradise. Tradition holds that they were later readmitted and became the darlings of the media when developers transformed Paradise into the Garden of Eden Motel, complete with a wedding chapel, hot tubs, a martini bar, and a cigar lounge.

A word of caution: beware of naming your children with thirteen letters in their names or they may be cursed. Think about it: Jack the Ripper, Charles Manson, Theodore Bundy, Albert DeSalvo, Jeffrey Dahmer, and the newest poster boy for evil, Bernard Madoff. And if you are addicted to crossword puzzles, try this one on for size: thirteen letters; clue, "Friday the 13th mass murderer." (The answer can be found at the end of this section.)

You can also try scrolling down to the thirteenth letter of the alphabet, where you will find the letter, *M*, which precedes some of the scariest words in the dictionary; *maniac, macabre, mutilation, mayhem, madman, morgue*, and my personal favorites, *mumps* and *measles*.

If you obsess about such things as I do, keep in mind that the thousand-foot-wide MN4 asteroid is scheduled for a close encounter with Earth on Friday, April 13, 2029. Finally the evening news will have an event to report that really qualifies as "breaking news."

Crossword puzzle answer: Jason Voorhees.

### Fear of Being Bugged

What has three letters and can be described as a computer defect, a hidden microphone, an ability to annoy, and an organism-causing disease? If you answered "A bug," go to the top of the anthill. Throughout the years there have been many varieties of bugs, including friendly ones, such as Bugs Bunny, the Volkswagen Bug, and, of course, Paul, John, George, and Ringo. There have also been unfriendly bugs, such as Bugsy Segal, Bugs Moran, and the surveillance bug.

The bugs that I fear the most are spiders, cockroaches, bees, bed bugs, and ants—and I'm not talking about my Aunt Bertha, Aunt Charlotte, or Aunt Jessie. They were scary looking but lacked the killer instinct, with the possible exception of Jessie, who looked like a grand piano, only with two legs, took no prisoners, and was clearly a person that you did not want to bug. Like the more petite ant, she could lift fifty times her weight and when intoxicated always fell over on her right side, often taking my unsuspecting Uncle Moe down with her.

While I am phobic about all kinds of bugs, ants pose the least threat to me, unless of course I am confronted by a colony of the dreaded red fire ants, known for their painful venom-releasing sting. The use of pesticides has been largely ineffective against these insects and has recently been replaced by the good cop/bad cop approach: first hit them with liquid nitrogen and then provide psychological counseling, and if all else fails, consider deploying anteaters, who have been known to use their snouts to suck in thirty thousand ants on a good day. Colonies of ants can extend for miles and number in the billions. That's a small number of queens supervising legions of disgruntled male workers, most of whom receive no overtime, have to contend with short lunch breaks, have limited health coverage, and die at an early age. It's not unlike today's society, in which women routinely outlive men.

Spiders are another story. Although curds and whey is not my favorite snack, like Little Miss Muffet I also have an intense fear of arachnids, especially black widows, scorpions, and, with all due respect to Fred Astaire, the fragile but menacing daddy long legs who, with three or four sets of eyes, is an ophthalmologist's dream come true. If you come across a spider sporting a red hourglass, it's unquestionably a deadly black widow, so give it a blast of Raid, and if that doesn't do the trick, do as I do and run away as fast as you can, because they are more dangerous than having Woodward and Bernstein on your trail. Scorpions, most notably the infamous deathstalker, love the warm weather and after a lifetime of spewing poison and paralyzing and killing their victims, many retire to the desert communities of Palm Springs and Phoenix, where they hang out under rocks and in the shoes and clothing of unsuspecting seniors. If you have curious youngsters in your family, it's always a good idea to have them check out dark places such as closets, attics, garages, basements, and under the bed before you expose yourself to these potentially lethal areas of your home. If they fail to return from their reconnaissance mission, you can always go to the Kids"R"Us Web site and order a replacement. They come in all popular shapes and sizes and can be ordered for next-day delivery. In a life-and-death situation, when immediate help is required, you can always try tweeting Spiderman.

Bees are another class of insects to be avoided. Don't let the fact that they produce honey and beeswax and play an important role in pollination lull you into a false sense of security. Until recently the threat of killer bees has existed only in movies such as *The Swarm* and *The Killer Bee Nightmare* and in supermarket tabloids. Now the threat is real as Africanized bees, who have set up shop in Brazil, are arriving in this country at an alarming rate, most without Green Cards or any signs of visible support, unless of course you count being bilingual. In southern California, they have been known to chase their prey for miles through the streets of Beverly Hills, past Santa Monica, and on to the beaches of Malibu, where media moguls can witness their vicious attacks from safe rooms. A word of caution: although there a few good bees around—the Green Hornet and the Bee Gees come to mind— but cannot be counted on to be in the neighborhood when the bees commence their assault. When William Shakespeare wrote "To be, or not to be," what he really meant was, "Beware of bees."

If you are looking to make a career move, join a pest-management team and become an exterminator. The job pays well and offers free admission to zoos, you get to wear a pressed uniform with your pet's name on it, and best of all, you ride around in a bright yellow truck with large bugs painted all over it. When it comes time to go into action, don't even think about reaching for a flyswatter; rely instead on your cutting-edge arsenal of infrared imaging, insecticides, and high-voltage electronic bug zappers, the no-smear, no-smudge kind, to win the day.

## Everyone is Afraid of Something

### Fear of the Big One

Most phobias can be attributed to a traumatic experience. My fear of earthquakes (seismophobia in medical parlance) is almost certainly the result of my exposure to the 1974 film *Earthquake*, in which the formidable triumvirate of Charlton Heston, George Kennedy, and Lorne Greene fail to prevent Los Angeles from being devastated.

My fear of quakes was reinforced years later when, without warning, I was tossed out of bed at 4:31 a.m., not by either of the two woman in my life—Phyllis, a five-foot, seven-inch sexy blonde (measured head to foot), or Gabby, a twelve-inch sexy Yorkie (measured head to tail)—but by the Northridge earthquake, which registered a formidable 6.7 on the shaker scale, a number that would surely have impressed Charles Richter. I have since learned that it was a magnitude 16 that wiped out the dinosaurs, so there is still an opportunity for the Big One to make history in California by eradicating large numbers of transplanted New Yorkers who now make their home in La-La Land.

Following this event, I sat down for a heart-to-heart with Gabby and explained to her that the past tells us that animals, especially cows, cats, and dogs, can sense and thus predict earthquakes. Any student of history knows that in 373 B.C., animals, including rats, snakes, and weasels, deserted the Greek city of Helike in droves just days before a quake devastated the place. Similar animal anticipation of earthquakes includes chickens that stop laying eggs, catfish moving violently, and bees leaving their hives in panic. So in return for including her favorite treats (chicken tenders) and Fiji mineral water in my earthquake preparedness kit, Gabby has promised to engage in excessive barking and erratic behavior at the first sign of the Earth's movement. We'll see, as only time will tell.

## THE WORLD IS A REALLY SCARY PLACE

My own earthquake kit has been thoughtfully assembled to cover the possibility that I could be isolated for weeks rather than days and includes a wide variety of survival supplies, including U.S. Coast Guard–approved vacuum-packed energy bars with a non-thirst-provoking formula and a five-year shelf life. Everything else—bottled water, canned goods, cookies and crackers, water purification tablets, batteries, vitamins, and prescription drugs— is replaced every three months. Why? Because I also have a fear of relying on industry-approved expiration dates that give unsuspecting consumers a false sense of security. The only items that are exempt from this ritual are lollipops, Viagra, and surgical gloves. I maintain three of these kits: the most extensive one for the house, a smaller one for the car, and a compact version that I keep strapped to my waist whenever I'm out and about. I still believe in the Boy Scout motto, "Be prepared," though my shrink thinks that my precautions are excessive. My rejoinder is that I think his hourly rate—his fifty-minute rate, actually—is excessive.

One of the possible affects of a major earthquake that I most fear is that all of my favorite hangouts—Nate 'n Al Delicatessen, Pico Cleaners, Dr. John Winters's Beverly Hills Small Animal Hospital, Koontz Hardware, Tower Imaging, The Ivy, Century Car Wash, Tony's Barber Shop, and Dr. Fishman's examination room—lie just above the San Andreas Fault line. I cannot begin to imagine what life would be like without my favorite haunts; it would be like relocating to Bakersfield.

Another frightening aspect of living through a major earthquake is the aftermath. I would be relying on FEMA to put things back together—the same folks who almost finished off New Orleans after Katrina struck with their unique blend of indifference, ignorance, and ineptitude. Do I really want to include FEMA on my speed dial and run the risk of getting a recording when I call for help, or worse still, actually getting someone from

## Everyone is Afraid of Something

FEMA on the phone?

Since I live on a hillside, another concern of mine is that when the "Big One" does arrive, a chasm could open up below and my house would be swallowed up by the violent upheaval, a cost-efficient albeit unique way to move my home to Beijing. The good news is that the booming Chinese real estate market is vastly superior to Los Angeles's—and after all, isn't it always about location, location, location? Another travel benefit would accrue to Angelenos following a major earthquake if a portion of southern California actually broke away from the continental United States and moved west, thus making it possible to commute to Hawaii in a matter of minutes.

I have discovered that one way to alleviate my fear of earthquakes is to have an insurance policy in force that will enable me to rebuild my house in the event of a catastrophe. But peace of mind comes at a price. Basic earthquake coverage is expensive, and here's the catch: it doesn't cover aftershocks—that's extra. So to ensure against hassles with your carrier, always remember to mail in your premium payment a full five business days before a major earthquake strikes. You'll be glad you did.

Finally, there are those who would like you to think that your chances of being murdered far exceed your chances of dying in an earthquake. Don't believe it.

# 2.

# Opting to
# Be Obsessive

*Perhaps it is only fair to admit that all phobias really are
obsessions too: if you're pathologically afraid of something, it's
hard to stop thinking about it all the time. Yet some phobias do feel
exceptionally consuming. When ordinary fear just isn't frightening
enough, it's good to know that obsessiveness is always an option.*

### Fear of Sleep

My abnormal fear of sleep includes difficulty in falling asleep,
difficulty remaining asleep, and the premonition that I might not
wake up at all. This last fear is sometimes referred to as the Rip
Van Winkle syndrome, although his nap only lasted twenty years.
Sleep historians contend that it was the smell of bacon frying
that awakened old Rip. Others insist that it was his ex-wife, who
tracked him down and woke him up to demanded back alimony
payments.

Preparing to hit the sack has for me become a carefully
orchestrated ritual that begins with the selection of a sleep window,
which in my case is 11:00 to 11:30 p.m. Before retiring to the

bedroom I always have a glass of warm milk accompanied by an Oreo cookie or two. While skeptics may frown upon the value of warm milk's slumber-producing properties, I have always benefited from a shot of moo juice, a practice that started 7,500 years ago in Europe, when pictures of missing gladiators first began appearing on the back of ceramic milk vessels. While taking sleep medication is another option, great care must be exercised not to use these aids if you plan to be at the controls of a Formula 1 race car, operate a wood chipper, pilot a low-flying crop duster, or engage in any activity that requires mental alertness—such as performing delicate brain surgery or proposing marriage.

After turning off all the lights in the West Wing, I head to the bathroom, where I methodically brush, floss, pop a handful of pills, and place fresh water in my dog's bowl. Gabby prefers Fiji but has been known to switch allegiance to Evian whenever she is vacationing in the south of France. Next I configure my two king-size pillows based on how much I have had to eat and drink. Since an attack of acid reflux can be a game changer, I tend to favor propped up over lying flat. I try to avoid watching the news, with its nonstop coverage of the most violent crimes of the day, and instead prefer to seek out reruns of *Seinfeld*, *I Love Lucy*, and *The Flintstones*. I have found that laughter is a better sleep inducer then homicide.

Once settled in bed, I turn the clock toward the wall to keep the room dark, activate the alarm system to keep out intruders, switch on my half of the electric blanket, and say goodnight to my two bedmates: Phyllis, who wears colorful PJs adorned with large and small dogs; and Gabby, whose custom-fitted jammies sport images of large and small people. They both snore and they each take up more then their allotted one third of the bed, making it difficult for me to get comfortable and fall asleep. Have you ever noticed that those who snore the loudest are always the first to fall asleep?

If I cannot nod off in thirty minutes, I follow the advice of the National Sleep Foundation and get out of bed to do something mundane and stress free, such as running the dishwasher or converting all of my usernames into Cantonese. No sooner am I back in bed than I begin to think about what horrible experiences await me in the darkened room. Will it be getting pounced on as soon as I fall asleep by something lurking out there; enduring a horrific nightmare in which I volunteer to serve with General George Custer at Little Big Horn, when I should have passed on the signing bonus and thrown my lot in with Chief Crazy Horse; or sleepwalking and finding myself in the window of Carroll & Co. the next morning adorned in an Italian black merino wool robe and receiving admiring glances from passersby? Another bedtime activity with potentially dire consequences is teeth grinding, which can lead to being outfitted with a budget-busting handcrafted nighttime bite-guard and, like Dick Tracy's nemesis Mumbles, being unable to speak coherently when talking in my sleep. I have also been diagnosed with Restless Leg Syndrome, which is best described as the sensation of having ants or other insects crawling on your legs. In my case it turned out that there really were bugs sucking on my legs, enjoying it, and telling their friends and relatives where I live and sleep.

Unable to overcome my many sleep-related paranoias, I made the decision to check into a sleep disorder center, where they conducted an overnight sleep study. Complete strangers with backgrounds as auto body mechanics proceeded to hook me up to sensors, clamps, cables, electrodes, and elastic belts. This is essentially the same protocol used to prepare doomed prisoners for execution but without the perk of a last meal. While it's possible to use the bathroom if nature calls, it's best to keep in mind that in doing so you will have to be unplugged and then plugged in again. For me, the downside to forgoing a visit to the loo is that it means adding bedwetting to my growing list of sleep disorders. Since the whole affair is recorded by employing multiple remote cameras, there is a high probability that I will be featured on YouTube's most-watched videos and as a result become a folk hero, making appearances on TV, scoring with girls half my age, and lining up book deals. Not to mention that, because of all the notoriety, I would be an odds-on favorite to become *Time* magazine's Man of the Year, which would inevitably lead to an invite to the White House and a chance to get a good night's sleep in the Lincoln Bedroom and thus be able to leisurely slide out of bed in the morning and hang out with the President and his family.

Keep in mind however, that if people were meant to pop rather than slide out of bed, we'd all be sleeping in toasters!

## Fear of Failure

My earliest encounter with failure was experienced long before I was able to spell or pronounce atychiphobia, defined by the medical establishment as fear of failure.

Beginning in kindergarten and throughout elementary school I was always fearful of receiving a dreaded F on my report card. It didn't matter whether the failing grade was for incorrectly lining up blocks so that they spelled RECESS, or for a deficiency in reading, or an inability to add and subtract. As for "works and plays well with others," my teacher even went so far as to suggest that I was controlling and bossy and must have my own way all of the time, which, as it turned out, was a reasonably accurate assessment.

Upon receiving my report card, my parents' faces said it all. I was told to go to my room, stay there, and never come out. In those days *never* wasn't really never, it was more like a couple of hours. It just seemed like never. After all, what was there to do in my room, without a computer, cell phone, iPod, or flat-screen TV? Not much, once I had flipped through a couple of comic books

41

and listened to the adventures of the Lone Ranger and the Shadow on the radio. I was told that unless my attitude improved I would probably wind up as a prison guard or a professional wrestler, or worse, an investment banker.

Many of my life's lessons were learned early on and had a sports orientation. It was better, for example, to play shortstop and bat fourth then to be labeled a failure and banished to right field, made to bat last, and forced to walk home alone.

Asking a girl out on a date was always a big risk—failure could occur in many ways. She could simply say no. The date itself could be a total debacle. As a result, while in high school I frequently had friends do my legwork and check out a particular girl. Was she available, did she know me, and if so did she like me, did her family have money, did her girlfriends think she would go out with me, how did she feel about a liberal Jewish New Yorker with minimal sexual skills? If the responses were positive, I would take the plunge and make the call, figuring the odds of this encounter not ending in failure were in my favor. For some reason I was always surprised when the girl answered the phone and said, "I was expecting your call, your advance team does good work."

When I reached the age of sixteen another potential scenario for failure loomed very large—taking my driving test. The peer pressure was enormous. To fail would mean riding my bicycle around town while everyone else cruised the neighborhood on four wheels. My only option would be to gather up my belongings in the dead of night and run away from home.

On the day of the test, I walked from the waiting area to my car with an air of supreme confidence, with my head held high—that is, until I realized I had arrived at someone else's car. Once I had found the correct auto, despite shaky knees, sweaty hands, a defective turn signal, and a stern looking examiner with gray hair and a clipboard sitting next to me, I somehow overcame my fear of failure and passed. With a national average pass rate of 42 percent I had once again defied the odds, thus enabling me to go home and unpack.

As I entered my freshman year in college I was faced with the task of selecting a major course of study, knowing that failure to make the right choice could have far-reaching consequences. After dismissing the most popular majors, Business Administration, Psychology, Economics, and History, I thought about rolling the dice and going for something unconventional such as Medieval History (good cocktail party conversation), Astronautics (an out-of-this-world experience), Computer Forensics (think CSI), Ranching (think Marlboro Man), or perhaps Gardening. Let me tell you from my personal experience with my gardener, Hector, that gardening can be a uniquely green profession in more ways than one. No dress code, no staff meetings, no corporate infighting, flexible hours—plus it's an all-cash business, and best of all, the possibility of failure is remote.

Ultimately I chose Communications, and early in my television career I was called upon to make a presentation for a new show—the first of many such pitches that I would make. In an effort to perfect my spiel, I rehearsed my delivery in the shower (sometimes without the water running), while walking the dog (and being constantly critiqued by her), parking my car (trying to ignore the incredulous looks from bystanders), standing in line at the supermarket checkout counter (and receiving a sprinkling of applause from sympathetic fellow shoppers), and sitting in the dentist's chair waiting for the anesthesia to take effect so that my wisdom tooth could be extracted.

I was overrehearsed and overwhelmed with fear and as a result the pitch failed to generate any support or enthusiasm. I viewed this experience as a lesson learned, part of the process of trial and error. And while many of my new programming endeavors failed, that was the nature of the business. A handful succeeded, and that was all I needed to carve out a successful career.

As I made my way into adulthood it was easy to understand why the fear of failure plagues so many of us: fear of failing at marriage, fear of being a bad parent, fear of losing a job or not progressing up the corporate ladder, fear of failing a stress test. Taking risks is one of the only ways to get ahead in life, and with risk comes the possibility of failure. I think that Babe Ruth said it best when he proclaimed, "Never let the fear of striking out get in your way." Clearly the Babe understood that failure is an inevitable, and essential, component of life.

## Fear of Making New Friends

A research study has revealed that a person's brain capacity can only accommodate 150 relationships, which is a drop in the bucket compared to the number of friends that you can accumulate on Facebook. Unless you make a special effort to categorize each of your contacts as "Friend" or "Acquaintance," Facebook doesn't distinguish between mere acquaintances and genuine long-term friends—not to mention frenemies, those people who pretend to be a friend but are actually your enemy. Included in this last unique class of humanity are insurance salesmen, politicians, telemarketers, blackjack dealers, and idea thieves in the workplace. My mother, who was quite adept at dishing out sage advice, always told me to keep my friends close and my frenemies closer.

Over the years my quota of friends, going back to my kindergarten pals and including a lifetime of people I have bonded with, has reached its cerebral limit. The challenge I face therefore is to selectively eliminate existing friends in order to make room for new ones, something that I am fearful of doing. I like to refer to this process as "the big goodbye." Discarding old friends can be a painful experience, like getting rid of old comic books, terminally ill goldfish, and my first molar, which was rejected by the tooth fairy as having no resale value.

I have a bunch of new individuals I would like to become friends with if only I could discard a like number that I no longer want or need and just keep my true friends—you know who I mean, the ones who will only stab you in the front. This practice is not as easy as it sounds, since there is a tendency to keep an old friend out of guilt or, in the case of my significant other, because she knows too much. In order to accomplish this downsizing I have placed several of my friends who are no longer relevant on Craigslist, where the listings are free and there are no commissions to pay. The only problem with this strategy is that Craigslist buyers are notorious for being unreliable, and after meeting my soon-to-be former friends, they might decide to return some of them. So if you try this strategy for friendship decluttering, be certain that your agreement always contains a no-return clause. I have also tried using eBay. If an unwanted person can be easily packaged and shipped, eBay may be the way to go. If you have any pint-size disposable friends, pack them in bubble wrap and send them on their merry way. It's important not to lose sight of the fact that friends, like animal crackers, come in all shapes and sizes.

What if you find yourself with available storage space for new friends and cannot find anyone who qualifies? What I do in those circumstances is push the envelope, and using the Internet and digital technology, create my own virtual friends. They are simulated beings who share my likes and dislikes, attitude and demeanor, and passions for junk food, self-hypnosis, collecting marbles from friends who have lost them, and experimenting with new sex toys. In other words, an ideal companion, someone who will always be there for me, and who, if it doesn't work out, I can simply delete with the click of a button and start all over.

When all is said and done, if I am unable to jettison my

nonessential friends, I sometimes donate them to Goodwill and take a healthy tax write-off, or if I am looking for value in kind, I might try to dispose of them at a swap meet. Who knows, I might get lucky and dance away with a worn-out stripper pole (strippers are extra), come away with a recent photo of Bernie Madoff lecturing fellow inmates on the fine art of short selling, or maybe connect with a rare set of reversible holiday lights—red and green for Christmas and blue and white for Hanukkah. If I cannot sell, trade, or barter my unwanted friends, simply giving them away is always an option and would certainly be preferable to taking a page out of the *Sopranos* playbook and using them as landfill. In the words of Jack the Ripper, "A good friend will help you move, but a great friend will help you move a dead body."

The Beatles said it best: "I get by with a little help from my friends"—especially the four-legged variety. As friends go, my experience has been that the best companions to have are dogs. It's a no-brainer: they are loyal, they enjoy Monday Night Football, and they never question your decision-making ability, ask to borrow money, or offer advice. They always leave the toilet seat up and the thermostat down, and they give you unconditional love. That's why they are known as man's best friend.

### Fear of Authority Figures

The dictionary defines an authority figure as someone who is able to command, influence, and exercise control over others. Marine drill sergeants, geriatric school-crossing guards, nightclub bouncers, menacing maitre d's, TV evangelists, and kidnappers all qualify.

When I was a kid growing up, parents and teachers represented authority figures for many of my friends. For me it was the diminutive, elderly matrons, aka ushers, found in movie houses during Saturday matinees. They were clad in white nurse's uniforms, wore white shoes and white stockings, and looked a lot like Mr. Clean in drag. Armed with high-intensity flashlights, they patrolled the aisles with a mandate to maintain order at all costs. Talking above a whisper, noisily removing a candy bar wrapper, attempting to escape from the children's section, and opening the side door of the theater to let friends sneak in were offenses punishable first by being taken to the manager's office for interrogation and then having to give up your ticket stub and any remaining Raisinets found in your pocket before being physically removed from the theater. I later learned that movie matrons received a bonus for every kid they subdued, searched, and shoved out the door. Many went on to have successful careers as prison guards, trading in their flashlights for stun guns.

Law enforcement officers have always intimidated me, especially those who ride around in squad cars and on motorcycles. The act of being pulled over and asked to produce your license and registration can be a nerve-racking experience, particularly if the car you are driving is from out of state and has been stolen. This scenario can be made even more daunting if the patrol car happens to be a K-9 unit with a ferocious canine behind the wheel. For such occasions I always carry a variety of freshly prepared doggie treats from the La Brea Bakery. I find that everyone is less confrontational when cookies are passed around.

My fear of law enforcement figures also extends to fictional cops, such as Dirty Harry, Joe Friday, Cagney and Lacey, and Sherlock Holmes. On the other hand, Monk, Inspector Clouseau, and Ace Ventura, Pet Detective, have never posed much of a threat to me.

The fear factor likewise applies to still or video cameras that have been strategically placed at busy intersections all around town. The bad news is that you will not know that you've been nabbed until a fuzzy image of you going through a red light arrives in the mail. The good news is that you can avoid detection by donning a disguise before leaving the house. I usually go out with red hair and fake freckles and make a funny face so that if I'm caught on camera I can claim it was Conan O'Brien who was behind the wheel of my car.

Authority figures who can be heard but not seen are another source of distress for me. The self-assured feminine voice that hides behind the navigation screen in my car has been known to display significant mood swings, sweet and reassuring when I follow her directions, hostile and demeaning when I stray off course. On one occasion she went so far as to reprimand me in front of my fellow passengers, blurting out, "Roger, what is your problem, are you incapable of following my commands?" Luckily I had my shrink's phone number on my speed dial and was able to receive immediate roadside assistance.

Among authority figures to be feared, judges rank high on my list and include hanging judges, divorce court judges, capital crimes judges, and the legendary judge Roy Bean, who held court in his own Texas saloon and dispensed justice with the aid of a revolver and a pet bear. He didn't hear many appeals. On the less-intimidating side of the bench are those venerable TV favorites Judy and Joe, as well as judges who preside over marriages, beauty pageants, and the contestants on *Dancing with the Stars*. And who can forget the fabled O.J.-trial–inspired Dancing Itos, who made it big on *The Tonight Show* and then, like a surgical scar, faded from sight.

As persuasive figures go, few wield as much influence as weather forecasters. We take everything they say as the infallible truth, even though they are wrong a great deal of the time. To get to the big leagues in the weather business it helps to have a name that will resonate with viewers and instill confidence. The names Storm Field, Sonny Day, Lee Rainey, and Snow White certainly sound more authoritative then Sidney Woppler.

### Fear of Making Decisions

Over the course of time I have had to make many important decisions. I have grappled with such life-defining choices as when to marry and when to divorce; when to buy and when to sell; when to have a sex change and when to stand pat; when to lie and when to tell the truth; when to gift and when to regift; when to play the cards I'm dealt and when to stack the deck; when to speak out and when to remain silent, whether to embark on a legitimate career or take an entry-level position with a major crime syndicate. I am confronted with decision making 24/7 and have come to dread it, which is why I am now clinically classified as being decidophobic.

Picture this scenario: I'm in the supermarket, shopping list in hand, and after a couple of false starts I manage to locate the peanut butter section. For the uninformed, it's sandwiched in between Smucker's jelly and Wonder Bread. What should be a simple selection process turns into a decision-making nightmare. In front of me are shelf after shelf of peanut butter jars: Skippy, Peter Pan, Jif, Goober—and they are available in regular, natural, organic, creamy, chunky, superchunky, salted, sugar-free, white chocolate, dark roasted, cinnamon . . . and for the deeply religious, kosher. It's not unlike paying a visit to Starbucks, where I'm asked to choose between caf or decaf, tall or grande, frappuccino or cappuccino, mild, medium, bold, or extra bold. Caving in to pressure to keep the line moving I decide to forgo the house blend in favor of the more exotic-sounding Ethiopia Limu, which I later discover is actually grown in South Jersey.

I wake up and remember that I have an appointment with the proctologist. I consider my options, to go or not to go. Since I've already cancelled three times, I make the decision to go. Arriving at her building (women make the best proctologists), I must decide whether to chance a panic attack by using the claustrophobic elevator, or climb the stairs to the twentieth floor

49

and risk going into cardiac arrest. I choose the stairs and take prolonged rest stops at each landing to catch my breath and reset my Global Positioning System. My NASA training kicks in and I realize that GPS does not work in stairwells. I'm off the doctor's radar screen, her office will never find me, and I make the decision to flee the building.

I enter a bank and there are long lines in front of each of six tellers. I don't like the odds with good reason. This is a game that I have played repeatedly and never won. I carefully observe the opposition on each line, trying to determine who has a single deposit to make, who is depositing the receipts from three weeks of retail activity, who is old and infirm, who is talkative (tellers love to chat with customers), who is trying to get away with depositing a check made out to a deceased uncle, and who is preparing to rob the bank. Woody Allen's bank robbery scene in *Take the Money and Run* flashes before me and I decide to come back at a later date with five friends. With one buddy strategically placed on each line, I successfully level the playing field.

Where to sit in a movie theater is always a tough call for me. I like to arrive early and lie in wait in a dark corner until I spot two small people taking their seats and then quickly move in to claim the seats right behind them. This technique does not always work however, since the diminutive duo may be forced to move if a couple of Lakers take the seats in front of them. Now the theater is filling up and I'm running out of options. I begin to sweat profusely, my pulse rate begins to look like my golf score, and the Milk Duds in my pocket begin to melt. In a game-saving move, I go to the manager's office and request a wheelchair so that I can sit in the obstruction-free handicapped zone. The downside to this gambit is that I'm so far from the screen that the movie looks like it would have on my 1952 ten-inch Dumont TV receiver. The upside is that I'm close to the candy counter and the Junior Mints, and in case of a fire an earthquake or a chance encounter with my ex-wife, I am just steps away from the exit and the relative safety of the mall.

When choosing a physician, there is much to consider. Does he look and act like a TV doctor? Do friends and acquaintances refer to him as "the biggest" in his field? Did he opt out of Medicare? Does the wait time to see him at his office exceed the time it takes to fly coast to coast? And does he take Wednesdays and Fridays off to golf with other AWOL doctors? If the answers are yes, put a line through his name. On the other hand, was he a veterinarian before he became a people doctor? Does he make house calls? Will he provide you with his unlisted cell phone number? And is he generous in dispersing samples of prescription drugs? If the answers are yes, he's da man!

Among life's most challenging decisions are where to eat, with whom to eat, and what to order. To be on the safe side, I always choose to dine in neighborhood restaurants in close proximity to the Cedars-Sinai Medical Center, establishments where the aroma of Raid does not greet you at the entrance and where waiters can recite the daily specials without having to rely on cryptic notes written on the palms of their hands. At dinner I like to be surrounded by old friends rather than interlopers who have entered my life through Facebook and LinkedIn. Menu selections can be a daunting task, and I enjoy bucking the trend, so when everyone else is ordering the healthy salmon I do what comes naturally and order the hearty meatloaf.

Remember that when trying to make a decision at a fork in the road of life, don't seek a detour—simply make the best decision that you can and move on. Or you can do as I do and go to your room, lock the door, turn out the lights, hide under the bed, and wait for the need to decide to go away.

51

## THE WORLD IS A REALLY SCARY PLACE

### Fear of Voting

I remember when Election Day used to be something to look
forward to. It was an excuse to take time off from work or school
and contribute to the democratic process. Well, it's not like that
any more. The last few national elections were so closely contested
and controversial that the average polling place, once a magnet
for community gatherings, has become as neighborly as a dentist's
waiting room.

My polling station opens at 7:00 a.m. and I generally arrive a
half hour early so I can be first in line. As I eased into my parking
space the last time I voted, you can imagine my frustration as I
witnessed a minivan discharging thirty seniors from a nearby assisted
living facility leisurely taking their place on line ahead of me.

Generally speaking, there is a prohibition against
electioneering within a hundred feet of the entrance to a polling
place. That means no campaign literature, political signs, or
photos of the candidates. I am therefore surprised to find several
sidewalk vendors doing turn-away business selling coffee and
pastries. Closer examination reveals a cleverly designed prune
Danish fashioned in the likeness of Barack Obama and an
equally imaginative powdered jelly donut bearing an uncanny
resemblance to John McCain, both in clear violation of the ground
rules established by the Federal Election Commission to provide
a nonpartisan environment. The early-shift poll watchers have
obviously missed their wake-up calls.

Once inside the polling place, I survey the physical layout. It's
your basic neglected garage, complete with oil slicks on the floor,
inadequate lighting, and furniture that would never sell on eBay.

Looking lost, I am directed to a long, narrow work
table, where I stand facing a team of election officials all wearing
identical red-white-and-blue T-shirts emblazoned with a caricature
of Uncle Sam pointing a finger at me and saying I WANT YOUR VOTE

AND I WANT IT NOW." The entire scene has the appearance of a court-martial proceeding.

Next a stern-looking woman wearing an I'M IN CHARGE button asks—no, *demands*—that I sign in. I comply and watch intently as she methodically checks the large voter registration roll, looks up at me, and dramatically announces for all to hear, "According to our records, you have been deceased for three years." The room grows so quiet you could hear a hanging chad drop. In an effort to resolve what appears to be a serious lapse in voter record keeping I produce a current parking citation, my Ben and Jerry's frequent-dining card (revealing a recent purchase of Chunky Monkey), and, to pacify the nonbelievers looking on, a one-time offer to have my pulse taken.

Satisfied that I am a living, breathing voter, the I'M IN CHARGE lady allows me to move seamlessly to the next stage of the process, the act of actually casting my vote. With everyone in the room observing my every move, I am introduced to the foolproof InkaVote Plus Voting System—no cards to punch, levers to pull, or touchscreens to touch. Simply a ballot card that can be marked with an inked stylus. Predictably, it is not as simple as it appears. Using a steady hand, the ballot must be secured over two red posts, which can prove to be extremely challenging for the Medicare crowd and anyone else lacking dexterity.

The next step requires the voter to resolutely grip the pen, much as a surgeon would grasp a scalpel or an ice cream counterman would take hold of a sugar cone and press down firmly to mark the ballot. Any deviation from this protocol will result in a mark that is insufficient to be read. A malfunctioning or leaky ink marker can also contribute to a disqualified vote and impact your dry-cleaning bill. Finally, you have to check your ballots dots. If they are messy, your vote may not count, and if this should occur, you can, under the Homeland Security Act, be stripped of your citizenship and immediately deported to a place where voting is not an option.

There is lots to do while inside the voting booth, including casting your vote for a wide array of propositions, ranging from the reform of standards for humanely confining animals to their respective farms to funding to ensure that owners of Smart Cars are as intelligent as their automobiles. All of this pressure-packed activity must be accomplished within a relatively short period of time, so you have to do your homework and come prepared. If you exceed your allotted time, a musical warning ("As Time Goes By") will be played, signifying that you have thirty seconds to wrap things up. Failure to adhere to this warning will produce unpleasant results—unless of course you happen to enjoy having a trapdoor open beneath you.

Our system is not perfect, but it's all that we have, and all things considered, a vote-by-mail ballot, while not as adventurous as some of the alternatives, might be the best choice when it comes to exercising your right to vote. The downside of course is that we would entrusting our votes to the U.S. Postal Service, which is like undergoing open-heart surgery at the hands of a surgeon who has just lost his license.

### Fear of the Truth

Because I fear the truth I have never bought into that old adage, "Know the truth and the truth shall set you free." Maybe it will and maybe it won't. Until now the only thing that has ever set me free was using my GET OUT OF JAIL card while traversing the Monopoly board. I'd rather go with Aldous Huxley's version, "You shall know the truth and the truth shall make you mad," or at the very least give you a severe case of acid reflux.

I would rather not be confronted with the truth, which is why when the mail arrives I make it a point to never open letters from the IRS (tax audit), doctors (lab results), my ex-wife (demands to send money), the FBI (an Academy screener bearing my personal watermark has been found in the possession of an Al-Qaeda operative), my brokerage firm (401k statements), a superior court (a traffic citation, complete with my photo, generated by an automated camera), and the vet (my Yorkshire terrier has not met her deductible and payment for her last round of life-enrichment therapy is now due).

As I am one who lives in constant fear of revealing the truth, it will probably come as no surprise to you to learn that I have my very own copy of the CIA counterintelligence interrogation manual "A Beginner's Guide to Strategies and Methods For Inducing Physical and Mental Agony." These techniques range from sleep deprivation, electrical shock, starvation, use of drugs, and the wildly popular sport of waterboarding to harsher measures, such as being forced to watch TV reruns of *To Tell The Truth* and *Truth or Consequences* and the threat of being released into the custody of your in-laws for the holidays. So don't plan to overthrow the government, and if you do, don't get caught.

The gold standard for being truthful was probably established by none other than George Washington, who in a moment of weakness, confessed to chopping down his father's cherry tree and under relentless questioning admitted that he did it for the cherries.

While I think that it's best to be insulated from the truth and live in a constant state of denial, the truth is that little white lies, left unchecked, can lead to a more serious condition generally referred to by ENT specialists as the Pinocchio syndrome, for which there is no known remedy.

Speaking for myself, I think that Jack Nicholson summed it up nicely when, during *A Few Good Men*, he turned to Tom Cruise and proclaimed "You can't handle the truth."

# 3.
# Technophobia

*The uninterrupted onslaught of new—and better!—gadgets provokes its own special terrors, today especially in anyone over the age of nine. Here are two of my pet twenty-first-century fears, one all-encompassing, the other more specific.*

## Fear of New Technology

I come from a world that was once populated by mimeograph machines, carbon paper, reel-to-reel tape recorders, cameras that required a roll of film, rabbit ears (not the furry kind), manual typewriters, vinyl records, small-screen televisions with picture tubes, phones that actually connected you to a live person without your having to endure a menu of endless prompts, 8 mm movie cameras, and television shows that had to be watched when they were scheduled for broadcast (no skipping commercials!). So is it any wonder then that I suffer from neophobia, a fear of anything new?

Today it's all about the Web and computers; machines that print, copy, fax, and talk back to you if you're lonely; CDs and DVDs (BVDs are out); TiVo, satellite dishes, iPods, LED, LCD,

## Technophobia

DLP, HDTV, and miniature camcorders; and cell phones that do everything imaginable for a price, including the iPhone. And let's not forget self-parking cars and talking kitchens that give you a heads-up on what foods you have inside your refrigerator and then prepare a shopping list for you.

When I have to rely on my nine-year-old grandson to explain the difference between a browser and a search engine, it becomes clear that modern technology is passing me by. I was the last kid on the block to succumb to the computer age. My skills, such as they are, enable me to access the Internet, email friends as well as enemies, and, if I'm lucky, bring up my favorites list, which as it turns out has nothing on it because I play no favorites.

When I encounter a problem that can not be remedied by rebooting—something we once referred to as turning a machine off and then on again—I call my IT specialist, who clearly regrets the day he offered to purchase, install, and instruct me on the use of my computer. Over time I have accumulated pages of notes on yellow legal pads detailing how to navigate my way through cyberspace, which as it turns out are quite illegible and thus completely useless. As a last resort I generally place a phone call to the manufacturer's customer service hotline, which instantly puts me through to a techie in, where else, India. These folks are available 24/7. They are alert, knowledgeable, friendly, and absolutely impossible to understand, unless of course you grew up in Calcutta.

I am totally phobic when it comes to adapting to any kind of new technology, and essentially the problem is my inability to comprehend the true meaning of the terms. In my universe, a *browser* is someone you might confront in a bookstore; *digital* is a form of prostate examination; a *cell* is a living organism somewhere in my body; *hard drive* means getting on the green in two; a *virus* is a bug that causes an illness that doesn't respond to antibiotics; *dot* as in dot and *com* as in comma are forms of punctuation; a Blackberry is something that you put in your cereal or devour with sour cream; Spam is a distasteful delicacy that I discovered while in the army; a *cookie* is a round, sugar-intensive snack (quite tasty albeit fattening); a *port* is a place to visit to watch the ships come and go; a *server* is anyone who will provide you with a menu and then take your order; a *worm* is something to be placed on a fishhook; a *curser* is an angry person who minces no words; a *desktop* is just that, the top of a desk; to Google is to fawn over a member of the opposite sex or alternatively a cute dog; TiVo is a Ringling Brothers clown who once befriended me; and we all know what a *mouse* is, a wannabe rat. And keep in mind that before Steve Jobs came along, an *apple* was something that, if you ate one a day, was guaranteed to keep the doctor away.

When it comes to new technology, laser eye surgery is another terrifying prospect. What's wrong with simply wearing eyeglasses?

Whoever coined the expression "Everything old is new again" failed to understand that everything old is, and will always be, old.

### Fear of Smart Phones

There are at least six billion cell phone subscribers in the world today—almost as many as there are people. China alone has more than a billion, while the tiny Pacific nation of Tuvalu is coming on strong with at least 2,100 (whose phones are all waterproof). These handheld marvels of technology aren't just for CEOs and gadget geeks anymore. They have become instruments to help the average Jack and Jill not only climb up the hill but also get the latest news, photograph police brutality, exchange emails with serial killers, play video games, download everything imaginable, and yes some enterprising women really do use their cell phones as vibrators while they are conversing. Talk about walking and chewing gum at the same time—and best of all, this can all be accomplished without using up your phone minutes. In a recent development, personal cell phones have also been modified to ward off muggers by serving as a stun gun with 500,000 volts of stopping power. Thus enhanced, they also come in handy in road-rage situations and when your significant other gets too aggressive.

While cell phones have become indispensable, they also have a dark side. Some evidence suggests that cell phones may cause brain cancer, induce ringing in the ears, contribute to loss of sex drive following lengthy conference calls, and impair the sense of smell. Supposedly cell phones also interfere with the navigation systems on airplanes, a theory that I have gone to great lengths to disprove. Following takeoff I retreat to the lavatory, where my experience has been that you can sometimes get a ground connection while flying below 10,000 feet, and I try to finesse a dial tone. When indulging in this dicey practice, always remember to keep the door locked, leave the faucet on, and speak in a low but firm voice. At higher altitudes I have often been able to talk with friends who are hanging out in lavatories on nearby aircraft. Bear in mind however that this technique requires a certain amount of planning, chutzpah, and a technical understanding of wind, cloud formation, and atmospheric conditions; it is a skill that I have perfected while spending untold hours as a victim of flight delays.

A word about cell phone etiquette. I consider myself to be a responsible cell phone owner, and like being a responsible pet owner, this requires a certain level of maturity and respect for others. I am therefore clearly in the minority, because wherever I am, be it a supermarket check-out counter, stalled elevator, waiting room in a doctor's office, bank, crowded bus, theater, or toilet stall in a public restroom, I am continually subjected to rude people, oblivious to everyone around them, taking loudly into their phones and intent on sharing the most intimate details of their lives. A hit man arguing about his fee, women graphically discussing their experiences with menopause, a stockbroker sharing insider information, a suicidal politician receiving advice from his ex-wife's shrink. You can bet that Darth Vader would have never condoned this type of behavior.

Have you noticed that the vast array of available ringtones can and frequently does shatter what otherwise might be a tranquil environment and how people let their cell phones ring incessantly just to show off their favorite ringtones? I have heard ducks quacking, dogs barking, birds chirping, cows mooing, frogs croaking, and my all-time favorite, a blue-throated macaw singing in harmony with another fellow parrot. Musical ringtones have also become pervasive. If any of the great composers of past centuries knew that their great masterpieces were being played over a cheaply made cell phone speaker and that they were being deprived of royalty fees, they would probably be turning over in their graves. Add to this list celebrity impersonations, cartoon characters, and a wide assortment of X-rated sound bites, and you long to return to the classic ring that Alexander Graham Bell had in mind when he invented the telephone.

My own cell phone skills are pretty much limited to making and receiving calls. Recently, while attending a screening of a yet-to-be-released film, I looked on with disbelief as a member of the audience was surrounded by law enforcement agents with guns drawn wearing those familiar FBI and SWAT jackets with bold white lettering to ensure that they are not mistaken for valet parking attendants. Was I witnessing the apprehension of a serial killer? No, as it turned out this individual had been fingered and apprehended for using his cell phone to illegally record a movie. This poor soul could have been thrown in jail, subjected to waterboarding, stripped of his citizenship, and made to eat large quantities of fruit Jell-O. Instead he was given the ultimate punishment, permanent loss of his guild card and the screening privileges that go with it. The moral of the story, don't get caught.

With all of my reservations about cell phones, my greatest fear is to be without one or, even worse, find myself in a location where there is no reception. This means I can never enter an MRI chamber, take up scuba diving, travel through a tunnel, visit outer space, take a shower, travel back in time, ski at avalanche-prone resorts, spend time in solitary confinement, visit Santa at the North Pole, or go parasailing. And since cell phones do not work at speeds over 450 miles per hour, being shot out of a cannon is out of the question.

# 4.

# Happy Days Are Here Again

*Holidays and special occasions of any kind induce their own special phobias. I'm even afraid of holidays I have never celebrated, such as Confucian and Hindu festivals, and afraid of ceremonies and celebrations I've never endured, such as the awarding of Ph.D. diplomas and ribbon-cuttings for pumpkin farms. However, I have not included all of those phobias below, because I'm also afraid of overwhelming my readers. . . .*

## Fear of Halloween

Over the years, Halloween has become an alarming experience for me, and while I have never believed in the mythical tooth fairy, I am convinced of the existence of ghosts, ghouls, goblins, zombies, demons, and all things that go bump in the night. It is because I have an abnormal, persistent fear of Halloween that I have been described clinically as being samhainophobic—I'm not making this up.

## Happy Days Are Here Again

As a youngster who reluctantly answered to the nickname Pumpkin, I found Halloween very confusing. My parents would say "Never take candy from a stranger" and then dress me up in an outlandish costume and send me out to ring doorbells and plead for *their* favorite candy. My marching orders were to fear girls, not candy. So mixed messages from authority figures figured prominently in my early exposure to Halloween. The result of this misguided parental advice is that I grew up having an aversion to candy and being frightened of girls (big and small). The good news is that since qualifying for Social Security I am no longer called Pumpkin, and when I take my grandkids trick or treating I always tell them to skip the candy solicitation and ask for cash instead.

According to folklore, the jack-o'-lantern, made from a hollowed-out pumpkin with a carved face, got his name from a scary man named Jack. No surprise here, since there have been many scary Jacks throughout history: Jack the Ripper; Jack Ruby; Jack Nicholson; Jack Bauer; Dr. Death himself, Jack Kevorkian; and the Jack in the Box CEO who, with a giant Ping-Pong ball–like head sitting atop a body dressed in a business suit, certainly qualifies as being more scary than a scarecrow.

Pumpkin carving, like rolling Cuban cigars or making a living as a blacksmith, fortuneteller, or professional mourner, is a very specialized line of work and not for the faint of heart. The first step is choosing a pumpkin that is visually appealing, deep orange in color, free from cuts, soft spots, and bruises, and has a stem attached. I have spent weeks at a time forgoing sustenance, sleep, and sex in order to visit pumpkin patches far and wide in search of the perfect specimen and occasionally finding myself trapped in a cornstalk maze late at night with menacing creatures lying in wait at every turn. This is not unlike trying to find my car in the parking lot of Dodger Stadium after the Old- Timers' Game.

Next you need the right tools for the job: carving knives,

a handsaw, chisels, drills, a melon ball scooper, marking pen, and the right size of candle. I always opt for beeswax candles, which last long, smell nice, and are environmentally friendly. It's also a good idea to keep a well-stocked first-aid kit nearby, particularly if you are going to burn your candle at both ends. From my own experience I can tell you that mohels, thoracic surgeons, and butchers make the best pumpkin carvers.

On Halloween nights I will sometimes take my fearless Yorkie, Gabby, on a visit to the entertainment industry's canine cemetery to visit the haunted doghouses inhabited by the spirits of Lassie, Toto, Rin Tin Tin, Beethoven, Benji, and Snoopy.

Halloween myths have always fascinated and frightened me. According to superstition, if you look into a mirror on Halloween you will see your future spouse, and if you have been drinking you will also see your future mother-in-law. Another popular belief is that on Halloween night you should not turn around if you hear someone's footsteps behind you because it might be the dead following you. On the other hand, it may just be a waiter from Mr. Chow with the fortune cookies you left behind. Another widely held myth contends that having supper in complete silence with an empty chair present will invite a deceased relative to occupy the vacant place at the table. If no one shows up, it's probably because they never cared for your cooking or owe you money.

If you are looking for a place to hang out on Halloween, you might consider Transylvania, North Carolina; Pumpkin Bend, Arkansas; Cape Fear, New Hampshire; Skull Creek, Nebraska; or Tombstone, Arizona. Personally I prefer the relative safety and comfort of my home, where I can catch a rerun of *It's the Great Pumpkin Charlie Brown*, watch *House of a 1000 Corpses* in 3D ZombieVision, be frightened to death by the quintessential slasher movie, *Halloween*, or just kick back and listen to Bobby Pickett and the Crypt-Kickers wail on "Monster Mash."

# Happy Days Are Here Again

## Fear of Reunions

The mere thought of attending a reunion sends me into a state of acute anxiety. Why would I want to relive the good old days with people who I didn't want to be with the first time around?

High school reunions come immediately to mind. When I first received notification that there was to be a gathering of my former classmates, most of whom I had not seen or heard from in decades, I initially rejected the idea, then considered sending an impersonator, but ultimately decided to appear in person. The event was to take place on a Monday in December, not at my former high school, where the gym was being used for the annual Audubon Society masquerade party, to which members come dressed as endangered species, but rather at a non-Zagat-rated kosher Chinese restaurant on Long Island featuring a $ 9.95 all-you-can-eat dinner.

Predictably, the reunion failed to live up to its hype. No one looked anything like their yearbook photos. The men sported balding heads, sagging jowls, and miniature hearing aids, while the women, who had been magically transformed into blondes, wore black to conceal their newly acquired girth and proved again why Costa Rica is the facelift capital of the western hemisphere. As evidence that everything old is new again, my childhood sweetheart somehow managed to squeeze into the same dress that she wore to our senior prom forty years ago. Caught in a time warp, I marveled at the fact that nothing had changed and that the old social cliques that existed in school still prevailed today. Without name tags, I was unable to recognize anyone, and so I simply referred to them individually as the cheerleader, the bully, the shy guy, the dream girl, the predator, the nerd, and the jock. They responded by calling me the class clown, which of course I was. The next time I'm curious about my classmates, I'll simply check them out on Facebook.

Family reunions are another event to be avoided, since they tend to bring together estranged aunts, uncles, cousins, and grandparents, all of whom share one common goal: to borrow money with no intension of ever paying it back. At a recent reunion I was designated to be the point person and make the keynote address. The event was sort of like a political convention but without the wild sex, behind-the-scenes deal making, and over-the-top media coverage. Finding missing family members proved to be a real challenge. A search of nursing homes, bingo parlors, and soup kitchens produced a couple of lost souls but not enough to support a family tree, or for that matter a family shrub.

To keep the costs down, we opted for a potluck dining experience. Aunt Bertha brought boiled flanken, a favorite of political prisoners in the old country; Aunt Charlotte honored us with stuffed cabbage prepared her way, with Spam; Grandma Sybil served her famous mud pie made with real mud; Cousin Phyllis pulled out all the stops and promised to bring us Shrimp Louie, except she forgot the shrimp and simply brought Louie; and then there was unpredictable Uncle Izzy, who contributed a case of 200-proof vodka that he had procured online from a small distillery in northern Siberia. The grandkids, Jason and Andrew, fearing a dearth of eatables, brought along a mixed bag of beef jerky, Pop-Tarts, Goldfish, chicken tenders, and leftover pizza, all of which they refused to share with the rest of us. The affair ended on a high note as I read off the names of the designated drivers and distributed eco-friendly, one-size-fits-all T-shirts with the inscription I SURVIVED THE LAST FAMILY REUNION.

One family reunion that it's best to stay away from is held in the picturesque region of Calabria in Southern Italy and features families bearing the names Gotti, Gambino, and Giancana. Making an uninvited appearance at one of these outings can get you into serious trouble, unless of course you happen to be Pacino, Gandolfini, or De Niro.

Over the years I have reluctantly attended all kinds of reunions, including military get-togethers, where, after dropping and giving him twenty-five one-handed push-ups, I felt obligated to salute my aging platoon leader, whose uniform prominently displayed twenty medals, compared to my one (for penmanship). There were also corporate revivals, where I had an opportunity to renew old hostilities with former business associates I still despised. Sadly, many of my old colleagues were unable to be present and had to text and tweet their greetings from exile, where most were awaiting extradition.

My experience with reunions has taught me that going back is bad, separation is good, and whoever tells the best story generally wins.

### Fear of Birthdays

According to historians who specialize in celebratory trivia, birthdays are a custom that originated in the ancient worlds of Egypt, Greece, and Rome, where it was customary to celebrate the birthdays of gods, kings, queens, and high-ranking noblemen, as well as orgy planners, used-chariot salesmen, and toga designers.

The first birthday I can vividly recall was my sixth, which was characterized by my receiving an unimpressive assortment of gifts not worthy of regifting; popping balloons in the shapes of exotic animals that traumatized me and turned me off from ever going to the zoo; a weird rent-a-clown, the antithesis of Bozo, who clearly had never made it to the top of the big top; and a scantily clad out-of-work chorus girl who erupted from my cake, imploring me to make a wish. It was the emotional stress of this occasion that contributed to my fear of birthdays.

One of the joys of birthdays for me as a kid used to be opening a greeting card and finding cash or a check inside, until one day, much to my horror, there was nothing but some badly written prose that didn't even rhyme. It was like losing a tooth, checking under the pillow, and discovering that the tooth fairy had eliminated me from her rewards program. The anxiety that continues to overwhelm me on birthdays can also be traced to my mother's playing the guilt card and constantly reminding me of the seventy-two hours she spent in labor with me (a footnote in the Guinness Book of Records), as well as my grandchildren's not having the time in their demanding school, sports, and sleepover schedule to call, and instead texting "happy bday gp pls snd $ 4 a new iPhone." It's scary, what the cyber revolution has wrought.

Unlike me in my growing-up years, today's kids are fearless and go to great lengths to celebrate their birthdays in style. Being part of the "party circuit" is a must, and in Beverly Hills offspring of the rich and famous get to star in their own themed extravaganzas in private upscale restaurants, complete with Vegas-style entertainment, gourmet food, lavish gift bags, and Annie Leibovitz, on loan from Vanity Fair, snapping photos. We're talking about the Ivy, not IHOP; Mastro's, not Mulberry Pizza; and Spago, not Souplantation. What ever happened to those intimate gatherings at Chuck E. Cheese's sans the paparazzi?

I can also relate to casualties of the calendar, including George Washington and Abe Lincoln, both victims of identity theft, who now share a common birthday on something called Presidents Day, a hybrid holiday concocted by the greeting card industry and lawmakers looking for additional time off from their legislative responsibilities.

I experienced another emotional setback when I realized that birthday cards designed for kids only went up to age twelve and that there were far fewer of them for birthday celebrants who qualified as being demographically challenged. The newest fad in conveying good wishes, the musical card, has produced such geriatric-friendly tunes as "The Party's Over," I'm Gonna Live Till I Die," "As Time Goes By," "Thanks for the Memories," "Staying Alive," and, as a reminder that I am approaching my Social Security years, the Beatles letting loose with "When I'm Sixty-four."

It never ceases to amaze me how many strangers know the date of my birth and feel compelled to send me a card. Among them are organ-procurement associations; the Neptune Society ("America's Trusted Cremation Provider since 1973"); alumni groups, including the one attached to a day camp I attended when I was eight years old; the folks at Forest Lawn Memorial-Parks and Mortuaries; and military organizations, such as the Salvation Army and the Veterans of Foreign Wars, which I find curious, since my service was limited to Fort Dix, New Jersey.

I'm also intimidated by surprise parties (what if no one showed up?) and out-of-work actors posing as waiters in steakhouses, surrounding and serenading me with an operatic rendition of "Happy Birthday" that would make Luciano Pavarotti turn over in his grave. While this is happening, total strangers at nearby tables feel compelled to join in the celebration while completely ignoring the pieces of lobster and the drawn butter cascading down their soiled bibs and onto their laps. Back at my table, a slice of flourless chocolate cake with a single candle has been placed in front of me as my friends cry out "Make a wish and it will come true!" Well, I wished that I was somewhere else, and guess what? My wish didn't come true.

I would like to ignore all of my remaining birthdays and simply concentrate on the important dates in my life: my next dentist appointment, car service, and colonoscopy. That means no recognition by friends, foes, family, and pets. My obsession with birthdays notwithstanding, I would like to live to be a hundred—that's 38° Celsius!

### Fear of Going to the Beach

When I was a kid growing up in Brooklyn, weekend outings often consisted of a trip to the beach at Coney Island. Back then the biggest threat to my well-being was getting lost on my way to the family blanket and having to be claimed at the lost-and-found booth along with the other misplaced kids, keys, and kites. You could always tell the net worth of those around you by the quality of the shoes that held down the four corners of their blankets. The economic scale ranged from plastic flip-flops to high-end Topsiders. Jimmy Choo had not yet arrived on the scene.

The beach scene was something to behold. There was music blaring from oversize radios requiring ten D batteries, smoke from open-pit cooking polluting the air and obscuring the view of the ocean, entire multigenerational families gathered under one beach umbrella in an attempt to escape the blistering heat, and dogs roaming around in search of a patch of green grass and having to settle for seaweed.

Fear of the beach and its surroundings began to consume me when I had my first near-drowning experience while trying to elude a monster jellyfish the size of a Hummer, which was followed by a close call with a low-flying seagull doing thirty-five in a five–mile-per-hour bird zone, and for good measure the sun's intensity had burned me so badly that lobsters from near and far were arriving to marvel at my appearance. The Palm restaurant even sent a waiter to check me out. While all of this was occurring, the lifeguards, who take a sacred oath to serve and protect, were out to sea. As horrifying as these experiences might seem, the worst was yet to come. It was called lunch at the beach and consisted of a tuna salad sandwich that was rapidly decomposing, chips that had long since lost their crispiness, and a large helping of Coney Island sand. After a while this unsavory blend became second nature to me, and to this day whenever I order a tuna sandwich, I always eat it indoors and ask my server to hold the mayo, lettuce, and tomato and simply bring me a side of sand. I was oblivious to the fact that, like chewing on a no. 2 pencil, eating sand can damage your tooth enamel and create dental bills that will lead to financial ruin and turn you into a beach bum.

Another beach-related fear of mine involves digging to China with nothing but a pail and shovel. On the plus side you avoid all of the hassle associated with flying, including airport security strip searches, lost luggage, contracting the flu from fellow passengers, negotiating with terrorists, and sitting on the tarmac for hours at a time with no air to breathe. Unless you hit a rough patch of shifting seismic plates, you can expect a smooth ride.

On the downside, the entire experience takes place in the dark and you could slip into a bottomless hole and go into a high-velocity free fall. This will cut down on your travel time, but you could get stuck in the inner core of the Earth with no food, water, cell phone service, or access to DirecTV. Even in the best-case scenario, you would arrive at passport control in Beijing and have to explain how you got there and run the risk of having your frequent-flyer miles confiscated. As challenging and uncertain as this passage is, it's probably not as harrowing as the trip from China to the United States, where it's all uphill.

Participating in a sand castle building competition used to be fun until, like Little League Baseball, parents began to take over the game. One afternoon I looked on with envy as a father introduced his kid first to a structural engineer and then to the architect of the boy's castle, I. M. Pei! As a large wave wiped out the moat surrounding my modest creation, I picked up my plastic beach tools and slowly walked away, only to see a huge construction crane coming my way with Donald Trump behind the wheel.

These days the risks of going swimming at the beach clearly outweigh the rewards. There are tsunamis the size of skyscrapers, melting glaciers that give new meaning to the expression "getting high at sea," runaway surfboards, garbage-patch islands created from discarded plastic bottles and other floating junk, and the prospect of encountering a Portuguese man-o'-war who got up on the wrong side of the bed.

A word to the wise: if you want to see Gidget, play beach blanket bingo, stuff a wild bikini, have a muscle beach party, or come face to face with Jaws, stay away from the beach and just go to the movies. It's safer, and you won't get tar all over the bottom of your feet.

### Fear of Daylight Savings Time

As all clock-watchers know, it was the esteemed New Zealand entomologist George Vernon Hudson who, while seeking a way to increase evening playtime with his beloved insects, first proposed daylight saving time (DST) back in 1895. However, we also owe a debt of gratitude to the author of the English proverb "Early to bed, and early to rise, makes a man healthy, wealthy, and wise," and to the inventor who came up with the idea for a flexible urinary catheter while twisting balloons into the shapes of exotic animals at a friend's birthday party. Although it's not generally known, Ben Franklin played a pivotal role in advancing the concept of DST after being told by his wife, following an argument over the family budget, to get out of the house and go fly a kite.

As mnemonic (rhymes with colonic) devices go, "spring forward, fall back" is one of the most popular memory aides around. It's in the spring however, when I set my clocks forward, that unpleasant things start to happen. To begin with, my birth certificate reveals that I was born at 2:15 a.m. on the date that daylight savings time springs forward one hour. But since no babies can be born between 2:00 a.m. and 3:00 a.m., the fact is that I really don't exist—a fact that my family patriarch, Father Time, rejects out of hand. Talk about an identity crisis!

With the arrival of DST I am overcome with fear of having to reset the dozens of clocks scattered around my home. I'm talking about all kinds of clocks: those on the walls; those inside kitchen appliances and electronic components; a grandfather clock (which provides sage advice along with the correct time); cuckoo clocks (with hip-hop cuckoos); clock radios; television receivers (one slip-up could result in *The Simpsons* not being recorded); explosive detonators (once my profession, now a hobby); programmable thermostats; the MRI scanner I recently installed in a vacant guest room (just in case); employee time clocks (to keep track of my expanding domestic staff); and, of course, my significant other's biological clock, which just keeps on ticking.

Then there are all of those clocks that are supposed to automatically readjust themselves, including my computer, iPhone, and iPad, all of which are synchronized to the mysterious atomic clock hidden somewhere out of sight at the National Institute of Standards and Technology in the foothills of Boulder, Colorado. I also have a sundial on my front lawn, which is maintained by my gardener, who has an uncanny ability to coordinate the appearance of the grass with the constantly changing position of the sun, a skill that he likely picked up from his extensive study of Egyptian and Babylonian astronomy.

DST also affects the biological rhythms of the youngest member of the family, my Yorkshire terrier, who no longer wears a watch, preferring instead to check the time of day on her smart phone. When Gabby's eat-sleep-eat-sleep routine is altered, the fallout is predictable: barking, whining, grumpiness, and excessive pooping, and then, as if to make a statement, a complete unwillingness to help clean up the mess. According to her therapist, a disruption in any high-strung Yorkie's carefully planned schedule can cause psychological and physiological stress, which is then in turn passed on to me and I in turn pass it on to others, creating a classic domino effect. I am not alone; many of my oldest farmer friends, including Old McDonald, have reported to me that they have experienced similar repercussions affecting their cows' milk production, chickens' egg output, and sheep's wool quality, and most importantly, their roosters' morning routine, since most of them are not happy about having to change their crowing times.

Since settings clocks forward can be a stressful as well as a frightening experience, I would like to suggest that we keep the fall ritual intact and in the spring set our clocks back twenty-three hours. Think of all the advantages! Rather than losing an hour of sleep, we will gain almost a full day of rest. It will be Saturday all over again. I'll never again miss the thrill and excitement of being present when the lawn sprinklers go off or watching the early bird get the worm or taking an eye-popping predawn hot-air balloon ride over Forest Lawn. Furthermore, if the Mayan calendar had been correct in predicting that the world would end on December 21, 2012, setting clocks back on the first Sunday in November would have been waste of time. However, in checking the record books, it appears that not all of Nostradamus's forecasts came true either. He predicted, for example, that Kim Kardashian's marriage would last three months. He missed by eighteen days!

Finally, as an alternative to having to put up with the anxiety that accompanies daylight saving time, I am seriously considering moving to American Samoa, where DST is not observed, and I can be close to my friends on nearby Tonga and the Cook Islands. The only downside to making this move is the pricey commute to the mainland to be with the grandkids at soccer games, camp visiting days, birthdays, graduations, and the day their braces come off, but since we all have access to Skype, why bother to travel?

# 5.

# Public Spaces and Shopping

*Psychologists simply subsume the fear of venturing out into the retail landscape under agoraphobia, but I think this represents a failure of diagnostic imagination. Shopping presents a rich array of subphobias, each of which really deserves its own name.*

### Fear of Buying a New Car

For me the decision to buy a new automobile is very much like scheduling a colonoscopy. It's scary to contemplate, requiring hours of preparation. It's fraught with uncertainty and so overwhelming that I generally put it off.

The car-buying experience is a necessary evil that comes around every three or four years. I always try to set the stage for the nightmare of negotiating with a salesperson by doing my due diligence. I log onto my computer and search for the type of car I want by accessing specialty Web sites such as Kelley Blue Book. What will it be—a sedan, coupe, convertible, Hummer, Mini, hybrid, or something even more exotic and intelligent then I am, a Smart Car? Above all, it must be a set of wheels that will impress the valet-parking crowd. If my car fails to make the cut, it's a given that it will be relegated to a faraway lot. Yes, there is a caste system among car parkers.

I believe that the car I choose should reflect not the lifestyle I am currently living but rather the one I aspire to. There is no sense in purchasing a compact when I fully expect to be able to tool around town in a Rolls.

It is essential to decide on the make, model, color, and price before arriving at the showroom, where I will be going head-to-head with the big boys in a classic David versus Goliath confrontation. The opposition is formidable: the owner, the sales manager, and right on down the food chain until I encounter the salesperson, whose sole purpose in life is to get me to spend more money on a car other than the one I want. I remind myself that the salesperson is not my friend. He/she is my enemy. I must prepare to be pressured, manipulated, cheated, swindled, and denied my constitutional rights.

It has been my experience that female salespeople are the most calculating and dangerous opponents. Their seductive appearance—black pantsuit, Jimmy Choo boots, lots of cleavage— is designed to lull the unsuspecting male buyer into a sense of false security. They have all the qualities of a double agent. Mata Hari comes to mind. The dress code for men generally consists of a well-tailored suit, white shirt with automotive-themed cufflinks, silk tie, knockoff Rolex and, in the Miami Beach area, a highly polished pinky ring. To round out the profile, add a limp handshake and a synthetic smile. If you recall the menacing look that the big bad wolf gave the three little pigs, you will know exactly what I'm talking about.

Upon entering a high-end showroom, the first thing you are likely to encounter is not a shiny new automobile but rather a lavish spread replete with bagels, cream cheese, Danish, and a staggering array of coffees. This seemingly innocent offering is designed solely to soften you up. It's not unlike a precision military operation: first comes the carpet-bombing, followed by the arrival of the ground troops.

It used to be that once I made my car selection and wanted evidence of its workmanship, all I had to do was saunter over to the vehicle and, in the best tradition of Mario Andretti, kick the tires, all four of them. The downside of this methodology is hearing the salesperson say, "You kicked them, you own them." Today's high-performance cars require a more substantial inspection. To fully comprehend the contents of the four-hundred-page, five-pound owner's manual, I'm going to need some big-time help, unless of course I happen to have a degree in automotive engineering from MIT. How else could I possibly master the navigation system, Bluetooth, intuitive parking assist, voice-activated phone, front and rear outboard seatbelt pretensioners with force limiters (handy if you are contemplating taking your car into outer space), and a first-aid kit that any major medical center's emergency room would be proud to call its own?

The moment of truth arrives when I meet my salesperson. His name is Arnold, but he says I can call him Arnie, which immediately sets off warning bells. We are not going to be pals. Arnie gives me his business card and asks for mine. I decline, fearing that acquiescence could well lead to identity theft. He tells me that all of the features can be mastered while taking the car on a two-mile test drive. I don't believe it and instead insist on a test drive to Palm Springs with a stopover at the Cabazon Outlets shops on the way back, so that I can combine basic training with discount shopping and lunch at the Morongo Casino, Resort, and Spa next door, followed by a couple of turns at the blackjack table. If I get lucky, the trip will pay for the car. On the way back to the showroom I let Arnie do the driving while I check out the fully reclining passenger seat and second-guess my ill-fated decision to let it all ride on the last hand.

Once I decide on the car that will be my home away from home for the next couple of years, all that is left to do is settle on the price. Predictably, the negotiation does not go well. Every good-faith offer I make is greeted by provisional approval, giving the appearance that the salesman is on my side. Reality soon sets in when I realize that my counteroffers are being brought back to the dealer hierarchy, who are gathered in a spacious, well-appointed room where they run the numbers while sipping double lattes and playing the latest NASCAR video game. A frustrated Arnie returns several times with pronouncements such as "You know the price I quoted you is below invoice, and we're losing our shirt on this deal," or "The numbers you retrieved from the Internet are all wrong," and the clincher, "Unless you sign the contract today, the car may not be here tomorrow." The large sales chart posted for all to see reveals that my salesman has not sold a car all month. The words *hungry*, *desperate*, and *potentially violent* cross my mind. Something tells me that now would be a good time to vacate the premises.

I tell Arnie that I'll think about it, which is not well received. He follows me out to my car, and as I drive away, the image of a grown person waving a white flag grows smaller in my side rearview mirror, where objects are supposed to be larger than they appear to be.

To maintain my sanity, I ultimately decide to use a car-buying service to find the car I want in the color I want at the price I want to pay, a much more civilized process with less wear and tear on my psyche. I wind up a happy camper, with the sobering realization that my car's value began to depreciate the moment

I turn on the ignition. Just think, in four years the Olympics will return, another election will be at hand, and I'll be in the market for another new car, older but wiser.

### Fear of Not Finding a Parking Spot in Beverly Hills

Webster's defines *parking* as maneuvering a vehicle in a space where it can be left temporarily. Sounds like a relatively simple thing to do. Doesn't it? Well, if you plan on parking your car in Beverly Hills, you will soon discover that it has become a nearly impossible endeavor.

For those of us who have not accumulated sufficient wealth to utilize valet parking, the alternatives are to use one of the municipal parking garages, try your luck at finding a vacant metered space on the street, call for a taxi, or stay home.

If you choose to ride and park, be prepared to drive around aimlessly and endlessly while consuming expensive fuel at an alarming rate. Also expect to experience numerous altercations with fellow drivers who are vying for the precious few available parking spaces. I have been cut off without warning, endangered by zealots making illegal U-turns, confronted with otherwise ordinary people standing or lying down in an open space until their friends or relatives arrive with the car, and my favorite, two automobiles each of which is occupying half a parking space with neither prepared to acquiesce. Even the arrival of Beverly Hills' finest, on foot, in squad cars, and on bicycles, fail to untangle this mess. Curious crowds of locals and tourists, many with a rooting interest, just add to the spectacle.

There are approximately 3,100 parking meters in Beverly Hills with most designed to let you park for twenty or sixty minutes, an inadequate amount of time for most of us. After all, where can you get a haircut and blowout in under an hour? Imagine the shock of seeing your glamorous next-door neighbor

80

rushing onto the street to feed the meter, dripping wet and wearing an ill-fitting salon gown. Suppose you run into someone you haven't seen in twenty years and you only have twenty minutes to get reacquainted. If you talk fast, that gives you a minute per year. Who wants to be placed in these kinds of pressure-packed situations? Predictably this results in the issuance of large numbers of parking citations, which represent a major source of revenue for the city. Then there is the proliferation of metered spaces that have been commandeered by restaurants, usually from 6:00 p.m. to midnight. Restaurants should be limited to no more than one metered space per establishment, which will undoubtedly prove to be troublesome for those eateries that regularly accommodate stretch Hummers and tour buses. On the other hand, those that cater to the Mini Cooper crowd should be in good shape.

Adding to the frustration of finding a metered parking space is the number of automobiles with blue or red handicapped signs dangling from the rearview mirrors of cars with occupants who, almost without exception, appear to be in excellent health. I once watched a dog limp out of a car with a handicapped sign and head straight for the front of the line at Pink's Hot Dogs for the sole purpose of socializing with the other dogs. When he returned to the car, the limp was gone. It is not uncommon to walk down high-traffic streets in Beverly Hills and find five, six, and sometimes even seven cars parked one behind the other, all displaying handicapped signs. Can there possibly be enough orthopedic surgeons and physical therapists in town to service all these people?

Furthermore, the dwindling number of available parking spots has been exacerbated by the city and special interest groups, both of which appropriate an alarming number of spaces for film production, construction, glitzy store openings, block parties, and tree pruning (which, oddly enough, appears to have evolved into a year-round activity).

# THE WORLD IS A REALLY SCARY PLACE

Here is a tip for you. If you arrive early at one of the outdoor metered parking facilities between Big and Little Santa Monica Boulevard. you may have an opportunity to park as a guest of the city. Simply examine each of the meters until you come across one that is defective, and then ease your car into that space and you are home free. You can always count on finding a couple of broken meters. If not, you may park for up to three hours, providing of course that you are in possession of twelve quarters. You cannot depend on the change machines. They are temperamental and seldom work. Furthermore, it is unlikely that they will dispense quarters, unless you are lucky enough to have a dollar bill that is in mint condition with a serial number ending in 711. If you do, insert the bill slowly with the picture of George Washington facing the Santa Monica Pier, and you may be rewarded with the sound of captive quarters tumbling into the change bin. The message is clear: most Beverly Hills residents would prefer to work in the entertainment industry rather than embark on a career as a meter maintenance professional (MMP), a vocation in which the likelihood of success is infinitely greater.

## Fear of Missing Out on a Bargain

When I first walked into a Costco mega store in Los Angeles I thought I had died and gone to heaven. This would be a shopping adventure unlike anything I had ever experienced. The array of merchandise was staggering and immediately rendered my carefully prepared shopping list, developed from a lifetime of trolling supermarket aisles, obsolete.

Starting with the huge but highly maneuverable shopping carts, which looked as if they had been designed by the same folks who brought us the Hummer, everything in sight appeared to be packaged in oversize containers.

Not wanting to miss out on a bargain, I decided to do a dry

run around the store to assure myself that I had seen everything that Costco had to offer before making any commitments. Two hours later, having completed my examination of the inventory, I ventured outside to the food court, where I proceeded to devour two hot dogs large enough to command special mention in the Guinness Book of Records. Only then did I select my cart, a late model with a built-in navigation system, satellite radio, and iPod. I joined my fellow shoppers, who appeared to be buying enough stuff to sustain them on a ten-year trip to Mars, where, I later learned, a new Costco outlet is under construction.

I started down the aisle displaying vitamins where I loaded up on large jars of vitamins C, D, and E, something called flaxseed oil, and enough Centrum Silver to see me through my nursing-home years. I figured that what I didn't use I could give away as Christmas gifts to the gardener, the mail delivery guy, the dog sitter, and the exterminator, to protect him against whatever it is that he might encounter while roaming around the attic.

My next stop was the canned goods aisle, to replenish my supply of survival food to get me through the next California earthquake. It was then on to paper goods, where I opted for the giant rolls of paper towels (thirty jumbo rolls), toilet paper (twelve megarolls), facial tissues (ten pack), and napkins packaged in bundles of 1,200. It was at this point that I discarded any notion of purchasing brand names and reached instead for every item that read KIRKLAND, Costco's house brand, which includes everything required to sustain life on planet Earth.

After picking up chicken, lobster, salmon, an outdoor barbecue to cook them on, a case of wine, two dozen bagels, enough batteries to run my Prius for the next two years, a high-definition television, twelve decks of Bicycle playing cards in case I am ever incarcerated and need to take up playing solitaire, a couple of best-selling novels, postage stamps that are actually cheaper than at the post office, a pack of forty-eight Snickers bars, a seven-pound container of Heinz ketchup, and flowers for my significant other, I headed for the checkout counter—but not before picking up four new Michelin radial tires, which I really didn't need but could not resist.

After paying with my brand new Costco card, I headed for the large utility vehicle I had rented for the occasion and for the next half hour I employed my considerable dishwasher-loading skills to carefully pack up the van, leaving just enough daylight to see out the rearview mirror. I was having second thoughts about passing up the opportunity to have my eyes examined but put it on my Costco to-do list for next time. One final stop remained, and that was to fill up on Costco gasoline, offered at a price too good to ignore, although my car's gas tank only had room for two gallons. Still, one doesn't walk or ride away from a bargain.

### Fear of Labels

My earliest encounter with labels was as a kid at sleep-away camp, where everything I possessed had a name tag sewn into it: shoes, sweat socks, shirts, shorts, sweaters, shark repellent and, as an aid to achieving All-Around Camper status, my bottle of steroids. For some inexplicable reason, these tags always contained my middle name, no doubt to set me apart from all of the other Roger Lefkons roaming the campground. These labels were highly durable and virtually indestructible, thus guaranteeing that they would stick with me through my nursing-home years and beyond.

This early experience led to a fear of all kinds of labels including those infamous mattress tags bearing a warning that unauthorized removal carries the threat of a stiff fine, or in the case of repeat offenders, a midnight visit by the mattress patrol, who will snatch you from your bed and see to it that you are never heard from again. My ex-wife was a casualty of such a disappearing act.

Sticky labels, the kind that you find on fruit, are not easily removed, and I have never been able to develop the skill set necessary to pry them off without also taking off some of the skin and thus exposing the inner fruit to prying eyes and a wide range of bacteria. Then there are those mysterious bar codes that you find on the surface of apples, kiwis, and kumquats. Sticky-label authorities will tell you that these codes reveal the price, where and when the fruit was grown, and its vital statistics, including the television viewing habits, blood type, and sexual preferences of the picker, whether the specimen was genetically altered, and if, when no one was looking, the fruit was sprayed with herbicides, fungicides, or pesticides, or simply left alone to survive on its own like the rest of us.

Labels found on packaged food products can be misleading, confusing, and intimidating. Nutrition labels are based on a two-thousand-calorie-per-day diet, which, of course, does not apply to the millions of Americans who are currently overweight, or plan to join the ranks of the obese by year's end. To fully comprehend the significance of USDA labeling on meat products, it's almost mandatory that you first have a master's degree in Food and Nutrition. How else to sort out the meaning of the stats on number of calories versus calories from fat—we're talking all kinds of fat—and details about protein, cholesterol, sodium, and vitamins? I'm also at a loss when it comes to grasping the implications of product dating labels, such as SELL BY, BEST IF USED BY, and USE BY. One false reading can land you in the ICU, where the only nutritional information you will need to know is what's in your Jell-O—plain Jell-O, not the gourmet kind with tiny pieces of fruit in it.

Other scary labels to fear include food-themed monikers for members of the mob, tough guys who answer to Cracker Jack, Meatball, Johnny Pizza, Mush, Stuffed Cabbage, and, as soon as he is released from the penitentiary, Gluten-Free. There are also labels

85

to describe people: he's not the brightest crayon in the box, she's a good eater, he's a mensch, she's a diva, he's a loser, she's a survivor, he's a stand-up guy, she's a looker, and they are both to die for.

Vanity license plates manufactured by the creative arts section of the state prison system are also of concern to me, since they provide complete strangers with an instant snapshot of who you are: CEREAL KLR, OCDMD, GODFADA, ODD CPLE, and LIC 2 KILL have all been spotted around town.

The recording industry is another source of label-induced anxiety. Benign labels such as RCA, Columbia, Capital, and Decca have, over time, been replaced by Asylum, Panic Button, Death Row, Black Eye, and Big Scary Monsters (a U.K. record label that released the debut single "Meat Balloon" by the band Pulled Apart by Horses).

Perhaps the scariest label of all is the sticker shock that awaits high-end new-car buyers. The Bugatti Veyron goes for $1.7 million, the Lamborghini Reventón can be yours for $1.6 million, and you can drive the Ferrari Enzo out of the showroom for a very reasonable $670,000. As you might expect, they all come with really thick payment books. My taste is a bit more modest, which is why I prefer to be seen in a stripped-down Hyundai Accent with a sticker price of $10,705—but if you buy one, be prepared to bring a portable radio and a battery powered three-speed electric fan with you.

### Fear of an Obstructed View—
### And of Being Denied an Escape Route

Once upon a time I was six feet tall. Sadly, I can confirm to you that the average person, although I have never thought of myself as being average, loses one inch of height every ten years beginning at age fifty. So at five feet, ten-and-a-half inches, I am fearful of not being able to see over the heads of people seated or standing in front of me at the movies, the theater, sporting events, parades, the circus, and in elevators, where I used to have an unobstructed view of the floor buttons and the all-important, potentially lifesaving red emergency button. Furthermore, it is scary to know that as I am getting shorter, today's crop of humans is getting taller. To deal with this growing problem, I make it a point to always arrive early for a movie in hopes of staking out seats behind small people, and if that is not possible, constantly changing locations as empty seats in front of me fill up with tall people or average-size people with big heads.

To further illustrate this phobia, allow me to recount a recent experience at the theater, which went something like this. A tall woman sat down in front of me with her petite daughter in the adjacent seat. I politely but firmly, with a menacing sense of urgency in my voice, asked them to please swap seats. After the initial surprise and outrage of my request subsided they did indeed exchange seats. My significant other then pointed out that the young girl seated next to me was now unable to see over the head of the woman who had been sitting in front of me. I said to no one in particular, but loud enough for this woman to realize our dilemma, that this poor girl, who had paid full price for her ticket, could not see the stage. It worked like a charm, because the lady in question spent the next three hours slouched down in her seat—way down. A classic win-win situation.

I am phobic about many things, but no fear is more compelling than the fear of being trapped in the middle of a row of seats if an emergency should arise that requires a quick evacuation. Those trapped in the middle seats almost never make it and simply become statistics. You always want to be seated on the aisle, ideally behind a short person. The same cannot be said when it comes to airplanes. If you sit in an exit row, which the uninformed consider to be preferable because of the extra legroom, you run a real risk of the emergency door handle moving to the open position while in flight and of being sucked out of the plane together with your seat. The prudent passenger always selects a middle-section aisle seat and in doing so enhances his or her chances of arriving safely.

# 6.

## Sick, Sicker, Sickest

*Fear of illness, suffering, and death might seem to be among the most purely rational of fears, and not truly phobic at all. Clearly, you haven't met my family. And above all, you haven't met me— and if you're a licensed member of the medical profession, you don't want to.*

### Fear of Germs

My fear of germs dates back to elementary school, where I once witnessed the school bully spreading his invisible microbes by deliberately coughing on the classroom doorknob. I recently came across his name on Facebook and was amused to learn that he is now the chairperson of the Health Facilities Development Corporation for the city of Houston.

Fast forward to the present, and my obsession with bacteria has turned me into a world-class germophobe with an awareness of the bacteria content of every item that I touch daily and a bumper sticker that reads KILL GERMS NOT PEOPLE. Because at any given time there are a hundred billion individual bacteria living, playing, and enjoying life on my skin, I feel compelled to wash my hands dozens of times each day for precisely twenty seconds, the time it takes to sing "Happy Birthday" twice. I adhere to this regimen before, during, and after meals; after handling a newspaper, using a telephone other than my own, or throwing out the garbage; preceding and following sex, even if it's with myself; and touching paper money, because it is made from a blend of cotton and linen that retains moisture and thus harbors *Streptococcus* and *E. coli*. I also make a point to never touch a faucet, hand dryer, shopping-cart handle, or ATM button without first slipping on a pair of surgical gloves.

Motivated by a need to survive, I have begun to make important lifestyle changes. To begin with, I no longer shake hands with anyone. Instead I pound fists. Traditional kisses have been replaced by air kisses, the kind you see when ladies do lunch. I shower three times a day, so rather than exposing my collection of Egyptian cotton towels to the questionable contents of my washing machine, I have resorted to using paper towels—the new thicker, quilted version. I have also abandoned my practice of sharing food, especially licking other people's ice cream cones, which, while economically attractive, is a recipe for disaster.

I avoid like the plague gas stations, airports, prisons, gyms, the homes of people I have known less than one year, and medical offices, with the exception of that of my physician, the highly regarded Dr. Fishman, who begrudgingly lets me use his private john as a professional courtesy whenever I'm in the neighborhood. A small price to pay for my not calling him at home or on the golf course over the weekend and interrogating him about various aches and pains I am experiencing.

When I venture outside the safety of my sterile home I always travel with my own supply of toilet-seat covers, antibacterial hand wash, minipackets of Kleenex, portable subway/ bus straps, and latex gloves, the one-size-fits-all model that comes in assorted colors to coincide with the seasons. To ensure that I stay informed of what's happening in the world of communicable diseases, I have the Centers for Disease Control Web site prominently displayed at all times. When things begin to go wrong, I want to be prepared, which is why during the past several years I have begun amassing large amounts of Cipro and Tamiflu capsules and hiding them under my bed, away from the prying eyes of my housekeeper and my dog, neither of whom has health coverage. While some might liken this behavior to OCD (obsessive compulsive disorder) I like to think of it as insurance against DOA (dead on arrival)

Germs can pose a threat without warning, so in these uncertain times, when biological warfare may be imminent, it is best to augment your arsenal of antibiotics, vaccines, and disinfectants. So do as I have, and pick up an approved biosafety level 3 protection suit. These garments come in a variety of sizes and colors. I opted for the Snowman model, white with black buttons. I suggest spending the extra bucks and adding an internally powered air-purifying respirator. The day that Armageddon arrives, you'll be glad that you did.

When it comes to a fear of germs, I'm in pretty good company with the likes of Howie Mandel, David Letterman, Cameron Diaz, Jerry Seinfeld, Matt Lauer, Donald Trump, and Mr. Potato Head. While we all worry about new germs, let's not dismiss the return of old favorites such as bubonic plague, cholera, yellow fever, Ebola, and just plain intestinal gas, for which there is no cure.

### Fear of Hospitals

My fear of hospitals has now reached the point where I am too scared to visit sick relatives and friends, unless of course they owe me money or have a great box at the Hollywood Bowl. Even though wonderful things can happen in hospitals (babies are born, people recover from illnesses, and miracles of healing take place) they are also places where people are ill, some are in pain and others in distress, some have unknown maladies, and many are suppressing anger and hostility—an experience not unlike having dinner with my former in-laws.

Given the likelihood of catching something that can be life threatening, whenever I visit someone who is hospitalized, I limit my stay in the patient's room and maximize my time spent in the one area of the hospital that is guaranteed to offer a respite: the gift shop. The beating heart of any healthcare facility, hospital gift shops contain a staggering array of merchandise, ranging from musical cards that play "I'm Gonna Live Till I Die" to stuffed animals that become aggressive and have been known to attack patients and visitors when served hospital food, Mylar balloons that will outlast your hospital stay if properly cared for, and exotic fruit baskets filled with lychees, pomegranates, goji berries, kumquats, and, for those with low testosterone, passionfruit. There is also an eclectic selection of books for those under the weather. Titles such as *Irritable Bowel Syndrome: An Insiders' View*, *A Funny Thing Happened on the Way to the OR*, *The Erotic Pop-Up Nurse Book* (also available as an X-rated DVD) and *Suture Self: The Essential Guide—Guaranteed to Keep You in Stitches*.

Visiting a hospital is one thing; being there as a patient is quite another. Over the years, as I have undergone several surgeries, my fears have proven to be more than justified. As soon as I settle into my room, I try to become familiar with my surroundings: the offensive odors permeating the hospital; the scratchy towels, cold floors, and sandpaper-grade single-ply toilet paper; people moaning in adjacent rooms—many of them visitors; nurses who don't look anything like the ones on medical shows;

congested hallways populated by patients on crutches, mechanized wheelchairs, and walkers, all talking on their cell phones as they try to avoid colliding with post-op patients parked on gurneys; and stained white coats everywhere. The bed, however, is a marvel, a Stryker S3, the Rolls Royce of hospital beds. Its features include one-hand operation of the side rails to help me deal with my fear of heights, specifically my fear of falling out of bed and plummeting two feet to the floor below. Next up is getting fitted for a hospital gown. I have never been able to master the technique of getting into one of these things and tying the strings behind me by myself. I always wind up putting it on backward and in doing so exposing my rear anatomy to paparazzi posing as window washers.

The day of my surgery arrives, and the removal of my gall bladder will be performed by Dr. Edward Phillips, who gained worldwide notoriety after successfully repairing my hernia during a power blackout with the aide of his cell phone flashlight app. We exchange small talk and he breaks the bad news to me that my gall bladder has no resale value. My last thought as the room grows dark is, Can I be certain that it is really Dr. Phillips behind the Ralph Lauren–designed surgical mask and not an intern in search of on the job training?

Back in my room following surgery there is activity everywhere. I am hooked up to a blood pressure monitor, an IV tube is hanging out of my arm, oxygen is being administered, a call button has been placed in my hand that plays the theme from Dr. Zhivago, the TV is on, and Hugh Laurie, aka Dr. Gregory House, is informing his team that the patient must have his tonsils removed before the next commercial break if he is to successfully compete on this week's *American Idol*. A nurse insists that I look at the "smiley-face chart" and tell her which of the six faces (calibrated from happy to frowny) best describes my level of pain. I go for number four because the mildly bemused face with a slightly constipated expression reminds me of Homer Simpson.

The nutritionist enters the room and tries to keep a straight face as she goes over the choices on the hospital menu. My experience has been that a typical hospital meal is a recipe for discontent served up on a decaying fiberglass tray: thick, salty broth like something made for political prisoners in the Gulag, tasteless chicken pot pie loaded with saturated fat and topped with a slice of white toast, vegetables boiled to extinction, and mushy Jell-O served with artificial whipped cream—is more than likely to exacerbate your illness. And don't be fooled by the misleading red "healthy heart" icons; all they guarantee is that the portions will be small but not necessarily healthy. If you are lucky, the orderly will place the tray out of your reach. Eventually I fall into a deep sleep, only to be suddenly awakened at 3:00 a.m. by a nurse closely resembling Nurse Ratched urging me to take a sleeping pill. My response is to throw up all over her.

When it comes time for me to be discharged, I'm packed and ready to go, gratified that my sell-by date had not yet arrived. With the requisite bowel movement behind me, there is only one final detail to attend to, the removal of the ID wristband I was given when admitted. Well, the bottom line is that it cannot be removed. Hospital security calls a locksmith (no luck), the fire department strikes out, and a team of NASA scientists arrives but fails to remove the darn thing after discovering that the bracelet is made from a combination of metallic rubber, medical-grade titanium, and kryptonite. Many years have gone by and the indestructible ID bracelet continues to adorn my wrist.

So the moral of the story is this: Since hospitals can be scary places, don't go there unless you have to, and remember that in a hospital, nurses call the shots. Also, it's best never to rely on a doctor whose office plants have died.

## Fear of Going to the Dentist

The panic and anxiety that precedes my visit to the dentist's office begins about a week prior to the date on the harmless-looking little white appointment card neatly tucked away in my desk calendar and intensifies as the day of reckoning draws closer. At three days and counting I begin to consider canceling the appointment. My excuses vary: an unexpected business trip, an invasion of termites requiring a team of exterminators, or my favorite, a case of lockjaw.

The receptionist sees through all of this, challenges my manhood, and insists on fitting me in later in the week. The trepidation builds to a climax the night before the appointment and becomes unbearable. I can't eat, can't converse with people, can't walk the dog, can't brush my teeth (it's probably too late for preventive maintenance anyway), and can't sleep. The only thing that can save me is a code-red terror alert in the morning.

Homeland Security lets me down, and so I pop a couple of Xanax and set out for the dentist's office. Because I have a chronic fear of being late for anything, I arrive at 8:00 a.m., two hours before my scheduled appointment. I spend the first hour downstairs trying to identify and evaluate patients leaving the office, many of whom are clutching their heads; some are crying, all are numb.

At sixty minutes and counting, I sit in the reception area with hands so sweaty I cannot grasp the seriously out-of-date magazines. My heart is pounding and I think I may faint. I make the first of several trips to the lavatory to urinate, a sure sign of either a profound nervousness or the initial signs of a major bladder disorder.

Finally my name is called, and I pretend not to hear it, as if I'm not there. I'm brought inside and placed in an ominous-looking contour chair with my head tilted way back. I complain that remaining in this position for more than sixty seconds will

95

trigger an acid-reflux attack and place stress on my herniated disc. No one pays attention. One of the two nurses in attendance informs me that X-rays will have to be taken before the dentist sees me. I remind everyone that radiation causes cancer, but once again no one pays any attention. Then the dentist arrives with a mask over his face, protective goggles, designer sneakers, and enormous hairy arms. Beneath the mask I feel sure that I can detect the signs of a disturbing grin on his face. Loud opera music fills the room. I am paralyzed with fear. He produces a needle the size of a Buick and proceeds to inject me with Novocain. I have a clear vision of the dental torture scene in *Marathon Man.*

As I brace for the needle to hit a nerve, I grasp for the arms of the chair and to my horror discover that this particular model has no arms. There is nothing to hold on to. I ask to get up to go to the bathroom and am met with a chorus of "Not now." The time is here. There will be no reprieve. My teeth are about to be cleaned.

### Fear of Taking Prescription Drugs

Imagine this scenario. An individual writhing on the ground is experiencing profuse bleeding, severe chest pain, nausea, sudden numbness, and breathing problems. Sounds like a battlefield scene straight out of *Saving Private Ryan*, right? Wrong. These are some of the side effects, described in a TV commercial, associated with taking Plavix, a prescription drug intended to reduce heart attack and stroke—if the consequences of taking it don't do you in first. And for dramatic impact, viewers are treated to seeing the subject being followed around by an empty hospital gurney. Get it? A heart attack waiting to happen. The only thing missing from this picture is Dexter, the loveable serial killer, lurking in the hallway.

As any student of minutiae knows the definition of Rx is derived from the Latin word *recipe* (the imperative form of the verb meaning "take"), and with almost four billion prescriptions filled last year, many with potentially deadly side effects, we are flirting with a recipe for disaster. Each year more than one million people are admitted to hospitals for adverse reactions to drugs, and of those about a hundred thousand die. If you are going to roll the dice, your odds are substantially better at a Las Vegas craps table.

It seems as though there are drug stores on every street corner competing for your business, and if you can't come to them, they will deliver your prescription drugs to wherever on Earth you happen to be, unless of course you are occupying space on death row, where sedatives are dispensed without charge—on a one-time basis.

It all starts with that little colored aspirin we were given as children. Today if your own genetics don't lead to your demise, the proliferation of drug messages is more than capable of doing the job. Which raises the question, why would anyone want to take a drug to clear up any health issue if it might kill you in the process?

The TV commercial proclaims, "Will you be ready when the moment is right? Not sure? Then ask your doctor if Cialis is right for you." After all, we are told, it's not for everyone, only those healthy enough for sexual activity. The good news is that I qualify. The downside is that the side effects are scarier than having an intimate dinner with Hannibal Lecter: a sudden drop in blood pressure; an erection, that, like an ex-wife seeking past-due alimony, won't quit; and vision changes that make it difficult to differentiate between blue and green, which will not create a problem as long as you don't apply for work at the Crayola Crayon factory. Not to be outdone, there is that TV commercial featuring an Elvis impersonator belting out "Viva Viagra." One side effect is sure to be the King spinning in his grave.

Our love affair with magic pills occasionally hits a speed bump when a painkiller drug such as Vioxx or a diet pill such as Fen-Phen is pulled from the marketplace. Nevertheless we continue to succumb to the media campaigns of the drug companies, which are only too happy to cater to our every whim, capitalize on every health fear, and get us hooked on one of their drugs for life. There is something for everyone: Claritin for allergies, Lotrel for high blood pressure, Xanax for anxiety associated with taking prescription drugs, and chicken soup for everything else. Popular remedies can cause a terrifying array of side effects, including hallucinations, coma, paralysis, liver and kidney damage, oozing of the eyes, and blue lips, which might not be so bad if you happen to earn a living as a clown. For peace of mind, do as I do and always keep a current copy of the *Physician's Desk Reference* next to the TV remote control. It could save you a trip to the ER.

The dire consequences of side effects are not my only concern, for once the actual prescription lands in the hands of a pharmacist, all kinds of things can go wrong. Pulling the incorrect drug off the shelf, giving the wrong strength of the right drug, an inability to read a doctor's handwriting, confusing your prescription with your pet's, suspect expiration dates, having your Rx filled by an unqualified pharmacy technician such as an out-of-work Wall Street trader or a terrorist seeking on-the-job training. And let's not lose sight of the fact that many of our favorite drugs and their ingredients are manufactured in places routinely monitored by our military spy satellites. You may also want to think twice about using a drive-through pharmacy; it's not the same experience as ordering a Big Mac and fries.

Finally, here is some food for thought. People take all kinds of prescription drugs, and those drugs go through our bodies and come out when we visit the bathroom. From there, they enter the water supply and end up coming out of the faucet we drink from. A vicious cycle if there ever was one.

## Fear of Food Poisoning

Most of us take the safety of our food for granted. Not me.

With *E. coli*, salmonella, and mad cow disease prominent in the headlines, is there any wonder that I lie awake at night agonizing about what illness I might succumb to as a result of ingesting bacteria? Summer barbecues used to be enjoyable, but now I worry that eating a hamburger might lead to a fatal brain-wasting disease, assuming of course that the toxic chemicals from the charcoal briquettes don't get me first.

I have never trusted those little USDA-approved seals that you find stamped on meat. How can I? Think about it. Do we know who works at meat processing plants? My guess is that the workforce is comprised of retirees, medical school dropouts, convicted felons, and out-of-work actors. I'm convinced that if you buy into the FDA-seal mentality, you will soon have your own case folder at the Centers for Disease Control.

Here's some advice. Never eat food at a hospital (even if you are a patient), a sports arena, an in-law's home, or from a street vendor, or food that is delivered to your home. And never step into a restaurant that has a rating other than an A. If you disregard this advice, you will almost certainly get sick, and depending on the dynamics of your immune system, you may die a slow, excruciating death, or at the very least you will no longer feel like engaging in sex.

If hostilities should break out between a waiter and me, over anything—slow service, a bad table, menu substitutions, stale bread (or worse, no bread), a dirty table cloth—it has been my experience that the waiter will likely seek revenge in the kitchen. If this situation arises, insist that the manager, or a member of his immediate family, taste your food before you do. As a hedge against the possibility of having to depart the restaurant without eating, do what I do, and have a meal at home before going out to dinner.

When I shop for food I pay close attention to seemingly insignificant flaws: a tinge of brown on a leaf of lettuce, hamburger meat wrapped with a loose-fitting shrink-wrap, a butcher with a runny nose, bananas without a Chiquita sticker. While navigating the supermarket you may be tempted to try free samples of those tiny giveaways; consuming these handouts can provide you with a one-way ticket to the emergency room, where they will happily pump your stomach and then send you on your way.

I have discovered that a favorite deception in food markets is to place all of the items whose sell dates are about to expire in the front of the display case. Most unsuspecting shoppers will fall for this ploy. To avoid becoming a statistic, always reach for the freshest products in the back and expect to occasionally come into contact with a human hand. The hand that feeds you.

One final thought: always chew your food thoroughly, and if you should find yourself choking on a piece of meat, take the time, but not too much time, to make an informed selection as to who will apply the Heimlich maneuver. It is counterproductive to survive a choking experience only to be hospitalized with cracked ribs, a collapsed lung, or a fractured vertebra. In order to enhance my chances of survival, I always select a table near the Heimlich maneuver wall chart. Be certain however that the instructions are in English, as most restaurants do not have an interpreter on the premises.

The same rules apply to pets that are choking on a treat, chew, toy, or foreign object. Follow my lead, and train your dog or cat to raise their paws in the air at the first sign of trouble. They will reciprocate by barking loudly whenever intruders attempt to enter your house in the middle of the night.

### Fear of Constipation

At some point in my past, there must have been an event linking constipation and emotional trauma, a real-life scare of some kind or perhaps a life-altering event, like being forced to eat calf's liver or taking a long trip in the family car with no rest stops.

Whatever the foundation of this phobia, my definition of a normal bowel movement is having a quick, uneventful evacuation at the start of each day, sometime between brushing my teeth and removing the bacteria-laden, insect-friendly plastic wrappers that encase my daily newspapers. I would never consider having a BM anywhere but within the nonthreatening confines of my home, unless of course I found myself in a combat zone. Fear of stopping up the toilet in a foreign location and creating an overflow or being the target of the prying eyes of strangers and contamination are, for me, major deterrents to taking this activity on the road.

An ideal BM, from inception to conclusion, should take no more than sixty seconds and not require extensive visual examination. In other words, it should be a well-formed, light-brown, odor-free deposit—not too hard, not too soft. Stool you can be proud of. It is essential to recognize EWS (early warning signs) that can spell trouble. These include muscle strain, cramps, the expulsion of gas, profuse sweating, shortness of breath, rapid breathing, nausea, compromised vision (defined as the inability to read small print, such as box scores, stock quotes, and obituaries), and an overall feeling of dread.

If a BM is not immediately forthcoming I have two options. Keep on trying until anxiety overwhelms me and I run out of things to read or simply give it up before complications set in. Here we are talking about rectal bleeding or the appearance in the bowl of a single, small foreign body, about the size of a lima bean. The sight of blood always leads to panic, even though intellectually, I know that it's probably from aggravating my hemorrhoids and not colon cancer. But can you ever be sure?

Fear of constipation, or coprastasophobia as it is known

among the medical crowd, always triggers a predictable series of proactive events. I exit the bathroom without looking back, begin drinking large amounts of liquids, consume lots of vegetables, fiber, and fruit, and maintain a caffeine-free diet for the rest of the day. A glass or two of prune juice, combined with the skin of the prune, looks and tastes awful but can be effective, providing of course that you can keep it down.

If by the end of Jay Leno's monologue I have still not produced a BM, I initiate Phase Two. This protocol consists of taking one red and white Colace softgel capsule, washed down with mineral oil and followed by the insertion of a 25 mg Anusal suppository. Sudden fear consumes my rapidly bloating body and I anxiously wait for daybreak. Obsessing over bodily functions is not a pretty picture and consequently sleep is generally not possible. If in the morning I am still chasing the elusive BM, I make my way to the medicine cabinet and quickly find what I am looking for, a Fleet enema. I always purchase a four-pack (Costco sells them shrink-wrapped). Be sure to check the expiration date: an out-of-date enema, even in a pristine box, can place you and your loved ones in considerable jeopardy.

A Fleet experience will generally produce some positive results, although they may not be totally satisfying. If more drastic action is called for, I once again pay a visit to the medicine chest and right behind the Vaseline 100% Pure Petroleum Jelly, I locate a set of three hermetically sealed stool sample test tubes filled with multicolored chemicals. Using a steady hand, I carefully place a small amount of fecal matter in each tube, shake vigorously— stirring doesn't work as well—carefully fill out the tiny ID stickers, and place a call to my proctologist, telling him to expect a delivery within the hour. As soon as his assistant hears me on the phone, she switches the call to voicemail. There are two possible endings to this scenario. Either everything is normal, or I will have to prepare for the unthinkable: a colonoscopy (a sigmoidoscopy is for wimps).

**Fear of Getting Sick on a Plane**

The spread of meningitis, tuberculosis, measles, and severe acute respiratory syndrome (SARS) are health issues that you would ordinarily associate with an underdeveloped country. Well, think again. With more then a billion people traveling by air each year, all of these afflictions can be yours; all you need is a valid boarding pass. Add to this list malfunctioning defibrillators, life-threatening blood clots, ruptured eardrums, empty oxygen tanks, and kosher meals prepared by gentile delis, and you will understand why I have developed an acute fear of getting sick on a plane.

Whenever I am planning to travel by air, the first thing I do is to use my contacts at area medical centers and the Air Line Pilots Association to secure the latest medical records and psychological profiles of the cockpit crew. Once seated in the aircraft, I always ask to meet the pilot so that I can gauge his fitness to be in command of the plane. Did he have a fight with his wife last night, has he consumed any alcohol in the past hour, and if so will he submit to a breathalyzer test, what did he have for breakfast, as a kid was he any good at building model airplanes, does he fantasize about being John Wayne in *The High and the Mighty*, and how many times has he seen *Snakes on a Plane*? Make a good impression, and you might be invited to sit in the cockpit, where pilots get ten times more oxygen than passengers.

Upon boarding, if you are greeted by a flight attendant who, instead of smiling, is blowing her nose, keep your distance and try not to get intimate with her when the cabin lights are dimmed and she places one hand on your knee while using the other to produce a touched-up photo of her adorable dog, aptly named "Turbulence."

Once you are airborne there is much to fear. A change in cabin pressure can cause motion sickness, bloating, cramps, and

103

middle-ear problems—and that's before you even reach cruising altitude. Once the plane levels off at 35,000, feet the sky's the limit. If I am seated near a person who is coughing and sneezing, I immediately deploy a surgical facemask to ward off dangerous organisms. These masks can be purchased at any medical supply store, and usually come in a variety of sizes, styles, and colors. Some are even available with funny faces painted on them.

A couple of dos and don'ts. Stay hydrated by drinking large quantities of bottled water. Avoid tap water, ice cubes, and empty bottles of mineral water that have been ingeniously refilled by devious flight attendants with bacteria-laden water from the lavatory. Do not accept a barf bag, pillow, or blanket. Smart buyers know that there are now reuseable airsickness bags on the market, some with clever advertising on them. Wash your hands at every opportunity and never use one of those awful scented wash-and-dry handouts, unless of course you want to have your tattoos removed. Remember that airlines mix recirculated air with fresh air, using a filtration system that is usually ineffective. So use your time on the ground to practice holding your breath for increasingly long periods, and before you know it, you will not have to breathe at all on flights lasting less than an hour. One more hint: do not reach for the free peanuts unless you are certain that you do not suffer from a peanut allergy, which can be fatal. If you are unsure, ask to be seated in a peanut-free row.

One of my greatest fears is becoming seriously ill on board, necessitating that the plane divert to an airport in a remote part of the world. New Guinea would be such a place, where the only doctors have the word *witch* preceding their name and they don't make airport calls, nor do they accept Blue Cross.

On long-haul flights, those exceeding twelve hours, I have been an advocate of having passengers suspected of being sick, and thus contagious, submit to a preboarding examination by a licensed physician. If found to pose a health risk, they would be placed in a specially designated sickbay located at the rear of the aircraft or, in high-risk cases, in the cargo hold with the exotic animals, contraband drugs, and stowaways. Those passengers who object to being quarantined would be denied access to the airplane, made to eat airport food, and face the immediate loss of all of their frequent-flier miles.

# 7.
# The Light at the End of the Tunnel . . .

*The ultimate fear, the final phobia, really needs no introduction, so you can just skip this sentence and move on the terrors below. . . .*

## Fear of Gaining Weight

Dining on rich food at every three-star Michelin restaurant on the planet has always been high on my "bucket list," but reality has now set in, and pork, pâté, and pastry have become passé. The prospect of having to purchase two airline seats, being unable to slide into an MRI machine, or taking up precious elevator space and when the door opens hearing a chorus of "We'll wait for the next one" has caused me to develop an acute fear of gaining weight, a condition I associate with people who haven't seen their feet in years. Obesity in the United States has reached epidemic proportions among adults, children, and even pets, giving us the distinction of being one of the fattest societies in the world.

Here are some of the telltale danger signs to look for. Are you prone to finishing other people's meals? Are you constantly topping off your gas tank just to be near the twenty-four-hour food mart? Do you spend all of your free time hanging out in the kitchen? Are you constantly on the look out for all-you-can-eat buffets? Are you addicted to the Food Network and its celebrity chefs, and when you are not binging, do you watch *Animal House* just to see the food fight scene? If the answers are yes, you are on your way to becoming an unhealthy statistic and a candidate for Liposuction or the more exotic gastric bypass.

Dieting can be a daunting task. Eating right means choosing tofu over Twinkies, mashed cauliflower instead of mashed potatoes, fresh cherries rather than cherry pie, popcorn not potato chips, and seaweed instead of sausage. It is also important to know your fats: saturated, unsaturated, trans-, hydrogenated, good, bad, hidden, Waller, Minnesota, and—my favorite—Domino, who is said to have had antioxidants in mind when he composed "Blueberry Hill."

Exercise is a key component to fending off obesity, and doing it at home certainly beats going to Gold's Gym and competing with the Muscle Beach crowd. The downside is that it's unlikely I'll run into Angelina Jolie, Jessica Alba, or Uma Thurman in my workout room. I have a treadmill with a high-torque motor, rack-and-pinion gear design, fifteen levels of incline, a built-in TV and DVD player, and a wireless heartbeat monitor. This modern marvel of engineering also comes in handy for storing books, CDs, old shoes, and unwanted presents waiting to be regifted. If you have the space and resources I would also recommend acquiring a high-performance ergonomic elliptical trainer. You can always substitute a human trainer, but make sure that if you do, he or she comes with PT certification from the Aerobic and Fitness Association (AFA)—not to be confused with the AAA or AA.

If you are like me and are obsessed with monitoring your weight, you will want to have an assortment of state-of-the-art scales strategically located in your home. They must be placed on a flat surface to ensure accuracy, so a visit to the local hardware store to pick up a carpenter's level may be necessary to guarantee that you have an even playing field.

My favorite weighing device is in the kitchen. It provides me with data on my body fat, muscle mass, and body water content, and best of all, it has the capability to announce my weight and that of my entire family in French, Italian, and Yiddish. In the bathroom I have an eye-level digital physician's fitness scale that is certified weekly by the Office of Weights and Measures. Rounding out the picture is a small scale in the shape of a dog bone for Gabby, my diet-conscious Yorkie, who like my diet conscious significant other refuses to weigh in unless the room is vacant and dark. Thank goodness for illuminated LCD displays. I recently informed Gabby that overweight dogs living in Los Angeles do not generally get multi-picture deals from major studios. That got her attention, and John Winters, our affable family vet, proceeded to put her on the highly touted Dogkins diet.

It should come as no surprise then that in the twenty-first century food has replaced baseball as our national pastime and overweight people have become the human embodiment of the dark side of our thinness-obsessed culture. Might the next step be government mandated "fat checks" for people over the age of six?

### Fear of Looking in the Mirror

There was a time when looking at myself in the mirror was a joyous occasion—not quite as satisfying as holding a winning lottery ticket, but close.

However, the aging process, together with decades of intense sun worshipping, has turned my once pristine body into a collection of age spots, funny-looking multicolored rashes of unknown origin, loose skin, and most disturbing of all, wrinkles—dark, bottomless crevices on the surface of my face.

Just as I can never pass a bathroom without using it, I can never pass up the opportunity to look at myself in the mirror. In recent years however, the fascination of watching my face develop blemishes has become a scary experience. The skin atop my eyelids has become puffy and promises to soon engulf the top portion of my eyeballs, severely limiting my ability to see.

Regrettably, the proliferation of dents has failed to give my face the character it deserves. Instead they have morphed from deep symmetrical lines of equal size on either side of my mouth to renegade fissures on only one side of my face, the left side, which also contains my only remaining wisdom tooth. Might there be a connection? Observing this steady disintegration of my face is beginning to resemble the horrors of *The Picture of Dorian Grey*.

As disturbing as some of these bodily imperfections are, they can, for the most part, be covered with clothing, pieces of milk chocolate, roasted almonds, and small containers of melting ice cream strategically placed. The deployment of these disguising devices generally keeps my significant other occupied while I make the transition from bed to bathroom, getting dressed or undressed. In the summer, shorts, bathing suits, T-shirts, and so on are a real challenge for which I have no viable solution other than to use that time of the year to undergo elective surgery, effectively keeping me indoors from Memorial Day through Labor Day.

Other than installing funhouse mirrors in my home and car, the only alternative would seem to be cosmetic surgery. But what if the procedure were unsuccessful? I could wind up looking like Scarface and sounding like Marlon Brando in the *Godfather*, and I could never get past airport security because my photo ID would be useless.

Acquiring a new face would almost certainly mean that none of my family or friends would recognize me, and neither, of course, would my dog. I would be an intruder in their midst, which might not be as bad as it sounds. I could pick and choose who I wanted to be with and spend endless hours going from bathroom to bathroom, humming "Mirror, mirror on the wall, who is the fairest of them all?" And the answer would be: *me*.

### Fear of Growing Old

Although, clinically speaking, I began aging moments after being born, the fact of the matter is that it wasn't until I received an unsolicited offer to join AARP, a brochure entitled "Medicare and You," and my first Social Security check that I really thought about growing old. Since that time, however, I have been obsessing about what it means to age, and finally I can see the light at the end of the tunnel.

As far as I am concerned, the fear of old age is basically the fear of death. I refuse to tell people my age, hoping that they will think that I'm younger than I am. I constantly think about dying my hair, having a facelift and maybe a nose job, and sporting a wardrobe consisting of designer sweat suits and state-of-the-art running shoes intended for people half my age. I have spent untold hours removing gray hairs from virtually every part of my body, including my head, ears, eyebrows, nose, and chest, only to see them regrow with astonishing speed. How this is possible, when I take great pains to surgically remove each individual root, remains one of life's great mysteries.

Everything about aging troubles me but none more than the health-related issues and physical deterioration that accompanies getting old. Recalling names has never been my strong suit, but now I am completely overwhelmed by the need to store and access myriad data, such as passwords, usernames, security IDs, account numbers, new ZIP and area codes, and my ever-lengthening list of prescription medications.

With senior moments occurring at an alarming rate and in order not to give the appearance of the onset of Alzheimer's, I spend a great many of my waking hours meticulously going through the alphabet in search of the elusive names of people, places, and things that I can visualize but not articulate, names that are always on the tip of my tongue. As a result of this mental anguish, I sleep less— about five hours each night, actually closer to four if you include the time spent traveling to and from the bathroom.

Fewer memory cells also means that I can no longer fool the folks at the Department of Motor Vehicle when I show up and am asked to read from an eye chart that I once knew by heart.

Deterioration in hearing and eyesight also contributes to my phobia. Whether I am watching television or sitting in a restaurant with a group of people, it's always the same: "Turn up the volume!" and "What did you say?" The good news is that my nearsightedness has improved. The bad news is that I can no longer read a newspaper or a menu without prescription glasses or the cheaper but just as effective magnifying glasses available for five dollars at drugstores and supermarkets.

With age comes the need for more preventative maintenance. I need a full-time assistant just to keep track of my medical appointments: flu vaccinations; PSA tests; checkups with my ophthalmologist so he can look for glaucoma and explain once again what floaters are; bone scans for osteoporosis; bladder and thyroid ultrasounds; colonoscopies; sun-damage evaluations by my dermatologist; thallium stress tests; dental X- rays and periodic cleanings; full-body scans which, I am told, provide enough radiation to light up the city of Cleveland for the Labor Day weekend; and let's not forget regular visits to my therapist to try to make sense out of all this.

111

Sex is not as frequent as it used to be, a sure sign of aging. Because of the wide array of self-help aids available, I must now first establish a window of opportunity, kind of like NASA preparing for a space launch. The phrase "Use it or lose it" has taken on new meaning.

My daily habits also have changed. Whereas I used to open the newspaper to the sports pages first, I now go directly to the obits section to be the first on my block to know who has died, at what age, and most importantly, of what. I've noticed a cause of death is rarely given for people over ninety-five.

Assisted living facilities and nursing homes are to be avoided at all costs. Without exception they are outrageously expensive, understaffed, poorly run, have no meaningful activities, and are populated by zombielike residents who exhibit zero ability to communicate. These homes are very much like Roach Motels: you check in, but you don't check out.

Senior discounts are almost nonexistent in today's world. If you want to buy a reduced-priced movie ticket, you must be prepared to go the your movie theater during the week (weekends are off-limits) between the hours of 10:00 a.m. and 5:00 p.m., and you had better be prepared to show proof of age. Looks can be deceiving. Early-bird menus at restaurants require you to be seated by 5:00 p.m. and finished by 6:00 p.m. Linger over coffee, and without warning regular menu prices kick in.

My experience has been that the only discount air travel seats available to seniors are the middle seats in the back of the plane, thus making long-distance travel seem like a form of incarceration. Friendly skies no longer exist for the geriatric set.

Growing old is not for the faint of heart. So eat slowly, lie about your age, continue looking for the Fountain of Youth, and remember the words of George Burns, who lived to be a hundred, when he said, "You can't stop getting older, but you don't have to get old."

## Fear of Poor Health

When it comes to health issues, my phobic behavior is off the charts. A simple blood test has become a challenging experience. First comes the decision of which arm to draw blood from. For some unexplained reason, the left is always a problem; as a result, the right is gradually filling up with small puncture wounds, and who knows what that can lead to if left unchecked? Once the blood is drawn, I remain anxious until convinced that the bleeding has stopped, for fear that the small incision from the needle might somehow enlarge and begin sprouting blood and become life threatening, requiring an immediate transfusion from an unknown source. I am also very concerned with the syringe. How do I know that it's sterile and hasn't been used before? Can anyone really be sure?

Because I take a cholesterol-lowering drug, I must have my blood checked every four months. Consequently, I have a favorite lab technician, and if she is not available, I will simply skip another pretest breakfast and come back at a later date. After the test is completed, I begin the follow-up process, calling the doctor's office continually until I receive a copy of the results and consult my extensive library of medical books and journals. The slightest deviation from the norm requires an immediate consultation with the doctor, wherever and whenever I can track him down—at the office, at home, on the golf course, in a restaurant. Doctors can run, but they can't hide. Some of my physicians have developed their own phobia, a fear of phone calls from me.

I am convinced that my pulse rate is a reliable indicator of how I am coping at any given moment throughout the day, and consequently I find it necessary to check my pulse at regular intervals to ensure that I am not at risk for a coronary or a stroke.

What I have learned from this process is that my pulse rate tends to increase dramatically while eating; having sex (or even thinking about it); opening the mail; entering the office of a doctor, dentist, or accountant; going through airport security; stepping onto a scale; being anywhere where my cell phone will not function; swallowing large pills that could trigger a fatal choking event; confronting any malfunction of my computer; and waking up in a hospital recovery room with no one else present.

Whenever I go out of town, it is with the knowledge that I am prepared to cope with virtually any medical event that may arise. What this means is having immediate access to an EpiPen self-injector and an ample supply of Benadryl in case I should I be stung by a yellow jacket, Klonopin and Valium to ward off the inevitable anxiety attacks, Nexium and Zantac to combat acid reflux, Biaxin and Cipro to fight bacterial infections, Lipitor to lower my cholesterol, Vasotec to bring down my blood pressure, Ambien to induce a sound sleep, a reliable alarm clock to wake me up from a sound sleep, Imodium for diarrhea and a Fleet Enema for constipation, Medrol for my herniated disc, Anusol for rectal discomfort, Orajel and toothpaste for tooth-related problems, Sudafed for nasal congestion, Collyrium Fresh eyewash to cleanse my eyeballs, an assortment of Band-Aids and bandages (some medicated, some not), two ice bags (large and small)—and let's not forget those old standbys Pepto-Bismol, Maalox, aspirin, Extra Strength (does anyone use regular strength?) Advil and Tylenol, throat lozenges in assorted flavors, Refresh Plus for irritated eyes, a portable blood pressure monitor, and a thermometer. Not to mention the names, addresses, and phone numbers of the major medical faculties in every city I plan to visit.

After checking each expiration date, all of the above medicines are carefully organized and neatly packed away in my carry-on, which never, ever leaves my sight. Speaking of sight, I used to travel with an eye chart, but after I had memorized all the letters, it turned out to be quite useless. I also carry two pillboxes with emergency survival medication whenever I leave my home, hotel, or ship's cabin. A note about cruising: you never want to be placed in a situation where your well-being depends on the skills of a ship's doctor—assuming that you can ever even find the ship's doctor.

It's all about survival, and there is no substitute for being prepared. Trust me when I say that when people see what I have in my carry-on, it's similar to the looks you would expect to get if you were trapped in an elevator at lunchtime with ten hungry strangers and you had the only corned beef sandwich, pickle, and Dr. Brown's Cream Soda.

### Fear of Running Out of Money Before I Die

You know the old saying, "If I had known I would live this long, I would have taken better care of myself." Well, if I knew when I was going to expire, I could eliminate a lot of my phobias. I would know when to stop having colonoscopies, when to fall in and out of love, when to quit working, when to cease paying bills, when to stop dieting, and when to get out of Fannie and Freddie, and I would plan my retirement so that I spent my last dollar just as I took my last breath.

Unfortunately none of us knows with any certainty how long we are going to live, and therein lies the problem. The good news is that overall we are living longer. The bad news is that many of us are going to run out of money, or worse, cash-equivalent credits, before we die. There is a financial term for this phenomenon; it's called "longevity risk." There is also a practical term: it's called "panic attack."

Sure, we can rely on actuarial tables to forecast life expectancy, but these charts are based on averages, not hard numbers. We can use the ages of our parents' demise as a barometer, but that's not foolproof. Or we can consult a

115

fortuneteller. In this regard, it's important to keep in mind that Chinese palm readers have a well-earned reputation for being more accurate than their Jewish counterparts, who tend to see things through rose-colored glasses—or without glasses, if they have had laser surgery. To my way of thinking, a more scientific approach might be to rely solely on fortune cookies, although you then run the risk of cracking open a cookie and discovering that it contains no fortune. How depressing is that? Perhaps the only foolproof method would be to pull a few strings and get a look at the Almighty's tome, which, according to Jewish lore, contains the exact date and time when we will all cash in our chips—assuming of course that we still have chips to cash in.

Job security has become almost nonexistent. You train for twenty-five years to do a job that has become obsolete, and then you train for another job that is outsourced to Sri Lanka.

The realization that your resources will run out too soon is generally accompanied by feelings of anxiety and worry and an overall sense of foreboding. This often creates a domino affect. First a lack of interest in sex, loss of appetite, an ambivalence toward personal hygiene that may include a cessation of removing excess belly button lint, and the on-line sale of all your remaining frequent-flier miles. Soon the urge to TiVo everything in sight will diminish and be replaced by a need to bend or even break the rules that govern our lives. One of the first signs of noncompliance might be ignoring the rules at the supermarket ten-items-or-less checkout counter.

As your net worth erodes, so will your ability to afford high-ticket items, ranging from a theater-size flat-screen television to imported chocolate sprinkles on waffle ice cream cones. Next to go will be three square meals a day, or at the very least a downgrade from Spago to the early-bird special at Denny's. Then will come the loss of heat during the winter and air conditioning during the summer, and finally total capitulation, in the form of the loss of high-speed Internet access. Reliance on food stamps, public transportation, soup kitchens, lottery tickets, and shoplifting will become ingredients for survival. Striking a deal with a local grocery store to purchase food items that have reached their expiration date will emerge as a viable option, and as desperation grows, you will be able to relate to Nick Nolte's character in *Down and Out in Beverly Hills*."

But don't despair, because once you die your worries about money will be over, unless of course you happen to believe that the reach of credit card companies extends beyond mortality.

### Fear of Having to Decide Where to Be Buried

As I grow older and the light at the end of the tunnel grows brighter, I find that my earthly obsessions with restaurant reservations, finding a good dry cleaner, and having a doctor who will write prescriptions with no questions asked have been replaced by a preoccupation with my final resting place. When life ends, as it does for most of us, I want to know that I have made the right, albeit the most cost-efficient, decision.

Being a traditionalist, my first choice was a below-ground burial, perhaps in my backyard or in the pet cemetery with my dog—anything to avoid having to network with complete strangers with whom I would have nothing in common. After extensive research however, I concluded that no casket is completely insect proof and that the imposing floral arrangement resting on my gravesite would not be sufficient to ward off scavengers in search of body parts that could be sold for big bucks on eBay.

So I considered the popular above-ground interment in a wall-like affair, but after further research I decided that being entombed in a concrete slab high above the ground would not play well with my sensibilities, given the fact that I am claustrophobic and have a great fear of heights.

As above-ground burial options go, it doesn't get any better than having your own mausoleum. Although I am not rich, famous, or a descendant of King Tut, I have always wondered what it would be like to be buried in my own crypt. Certainly it has advantages: it's maintenance free, more comfortable to visit in inclement weather, and a classy place to spend eternity. Being entombed in my own personalized private estate would also be symbolic of the noble principles that have characterized my life—excluding of course things like avoiding jury duty, failing to pay parking tickets, taking questionable deductions on my tax returns, and faking orgasms. For the sake of appearances, I would need a family coat of arms, a plant service, a glass skylight, cross ventilation, round-the-clock security, and the technology to permit visitors, using a handheld device, to retrieve photos and recorded messages from my mortal years. So in death I would still be able to tell my significant other, "Hurry up and get dressed or we'll be late." Alas, when I finally added up all of the basic costs plus the bells and whistles, it became clear to me that although it's good to be king, I was not in the same league as the pharaohs.

Seeking alternatives, I came across an ad by a hot new company that offered a dignified $484.00 cremation. This outfit had a policy of only cremating human remains (no commingling with the ashes of goats, lizards, birds, or space aliens), guaranteed to cremate only one person at a time (group therapy is one thing, but a group cremation would definitely be a stretch), and offered to make things right if they failed to live up to expectations, which struck me as being a half-baked commitment. While the notion of scattering my ashes to the four winds or resting comfortably in a colorful vase for all to see had some appeal, the vision of my friends and relatives moving on to an afterlife with all of their body parts intact while I lay in ruins like Humpty Dumpty proved to be a deal breaker.

I briefly considered cryogenics, but the cost to be maintained in a prolonged frozen state turned out to be prohibitive. If the wait for a cure for whatever had done me in exceeded my financial resources, I would be giving new meaning to the phrase *having a meltdown*.

A do it yourself eco-friendly funeral at sea sounded glamorous and cheap and would relieve my loved ones of the obligation to periodically visit me unless, of course, it turned out that a member of my family was an expert on tides. Furthermore, everything I needed to know was available in a planning kit that could be viewed online and included the best times to schedule a sailing, how to write a eulogy, prayers, and music, and best of all, copies of all the Environmental Protection Agency forms required to make it legal. (You must be three nautical miles from land and at a depth of 600 feet.) I would need a specially constructed coffin to ensure a quick descent so as not to end up floating to the surface at an inopportune time and ruining everyone's buffet lunch.

There is a downside however. If it turned out that I was murdered by a distraught woman, my body could not be exhumed for an autopsy. I was also turned off by the possibility that if in fact I was not quite deceased, my inability to swim could result in my drowning. Then there is the class of people you run into on the ocean floor. Let's not forget that Salvatore "Big Pussy" Bonpensiero was killed and then buried at sea in the last episode of the second season of the *The Sopranos*. Sleeping with the fishes is one thing, hanging out with Big Pussy is another.

At the end of the day, I think I would opt not to die at all but simply be placed on a life-support system with DirecTV with high-definition capability. The hospital staff would keep an eye on me, my friends and relatives would come and go—as would people I owed money to—and I would simply lie on my Tempur-Pedic mattress and goose-down pillows and wait it out. After all, everyone knows that all good things come to those who wait.

# Afterword

# Starting Over, or, My Dog Has Inherited My Phobias

Gabby is my Yorkshire terrier. When we first met she was eight weeks old—fifty-six weeks if you rely on the human-to-dog-years conversion table. She was cute, even-tempered, devoid of any neurosis, and friendly with other dogs and most humans her size, had not yet figured out the difference between a treat and a chew toy, and was not dependent on Prozac to get her through the day. Fast-forward six years and what we have is a phobic dog–father relationship. Not a pretty picture. Gabby, who is still cute, has figured out that every discharge of her bodily waste triggers a reward, and so she carefully parcels it out throughout the day and night at regular intervals.

She shares my bed, arises at 6:00 a.m. and immediately begins licking my face relentlessly, sure that her will is greater than mine, that my pretending to be asleep is simply a ploy, and that sooner rather than later, I will get out of bed and follow her into the kitchen, where she will be rewarded with a serving of Wellness Complete Health Super5Mix. I always give her the same number of pieces, twelve, which must all be the same size. Broken or irregularly shaped pieces are not acceptable and are always discarded.

## Afterword

Fearful that I will be the cause of some misfortune lurking in her path, I monitor Gabby throughout the day as if she were in an intensive-care unit. At the slightest sign of trouble—wheezing, coughing, sneezing, whining, an irregular heartbeat, not eating her meticulously prepared high-end food—it's off to the vet.

I always call ahead so they know we are coming and our arrival is not unlike a scene out of *MASH*. There are frequent visits to the vet, and although we are on the family plan, there are no real discounts. I have my vet's cell-phone and office numbers; I know where he goes to get gas, play golf, and pick up his dry cleaning. I also know his favorite restaurants and closest friends and relatives. There is no escape.

Gabby and I navigate our way through life as one. When I have my teeth cleaned, she has hers cleaned. When she gets her shots, I get mine. When I have my haircut, she gets groomed. When we go for a walk, she leads and I follow, and both of us avoid stepping on the cracks in the sidewalk—something I picked up from her.

We have learned from one another. I bark at customer service people at the cable company, telephone company, Social Security office, banks, and department stores. Gabby barks at dogs and people her size, and cars, birds, and any sounds she cannot readily identify. Even in dog years, she is too young to bark at the Social Security reps.

Together we have become a dynamic duo, nervous, suspicious, high-strung, insecure, materialistic, and afraid of the dark and of meeting new people. And since we live near the San Andreas Fault, we are always fearful that the Big One is just around the corner.

For better or worse, we have bonded for all eternity, and if there is an afterlife, we will probably return as Roger and Gabby, only with our roles reversed.

121

# Acknowledgments

I am indebted to the many people who, through their encouragement and guidance, have enabled me to share with you the inner workings of my phobic world. The list includes family, friends, schoolmates, business colleagues, physicians, enemies past and present, and those who, in a moment of weakness, let me borrow money knowing full well they would never see a dime returned.

To begin with I want to thank Phyllis Klein, my partner in life, whose love and support inspired me to write about my many phobias, most of which she has had an opportunity to observe close up. Without her at my side, writing this account of my phobic behavior would still be on my bucket list.

I thank my sister in-law, Wendy, and my brother, Harris, who contributed mightily to assembling this book and who reinforced my desire to share my neuroses with others as an alternative to embarking on a life of crime—which still remains an option.

John Seitz, whose skills as editor of the *Beverly Hills Courier* and as a PR maven rubbed off and enabled me to say in a couple of words what heretofore had required several sentences. I'll always be grateful, John.

My thanks to a couple of comedy legends, Budd Friedman and David Steinberg for recognizing me as a true neurotic and for their friendship, support, and encouragement.

I appreciate the input of Sybil Goldrich, activist and actress, who I have known since my high school days and who over the years has been entertained by everything I have written, with the exception of the time that I compared her pot roast to the food served to political prisoners in labor camps.

122

I thank noted novelist and raconteur Stephen Maitland-Lewis and his awesome wife, Joni Berry, for continuing to support my literary efforts. With us it's a mutual lovefest.

Legendary radio personality Bruce "Cousin Brucie" Morrow and his terrific wife, Jodie, whose friendship and backing over the years have inspired me to come clean about my phobias and share them with a larger audience. Thanks, Bruce!

My gratitude goes to TV personality, and friend Christine Schwab, who acted as a mentor, although not fully understanding my fear of the dark until one night when she experienced a power failure and had to resort to using birthday candles to find her way around the house.

Dr. Louis Fishman deserves a giant thank you. He has sought to find a medical explanation for my neurotic behavior while encouraging me to continue to write about my phobias, most notably my fear of getting sick on the weekend and not being able to track him down on the golf course.

I thank John Terenzio, renowned TV producer and friend of many years, who once said to me, "If you have a fear of getting sick on a plane, go sit next to my wife, Denise."

I'm appreciative of Rabbi Sanford Shapero, a marvelous dinner companion and deeply religious person, who inspires me and continues to advocate that I look within to overcome my phobias, not realizing that I suffer from a fear of confined spaces that makes such self-examination impossible.

Celebrated sports personality Marv Albert has been very encouraging. When asked if I should write a book about my phobias, he replied enthusiastically, "Yes!"

A well-earned thank you goes to Gloria Heidi and Robert Adams for recognizing me for the genius that I am and never missing an opportunity to provide encouragement, preferably over lunch.

I appreciate my tennis buddies, Howard Storm, Michael Callen, and Roger Federer, who understand that when I call a ball out when it is really in, it's only because of my fear of losing.

My thanks to Ed Ferman, my high school partner in crime and himself a publisher, for his backing over the years.

A tip of the hat to Ave Butensky for motivating me to write and publish this book. My only regret is that he now shows signs of having contracted many of my phobias.

I thank Bob and Amy Katz, who helped me overcome my fear of water by inviting me out on their boat and then running it aground in Long Island Sound. Luckily I had the Coast Guard's unlisted number on my speed dial.

A big thank you to Dr. John Winters, preeminent veterinarian to the stars, for his enthusiastic response to my writing and for including my Yorkie, Gabby, among his inner circle of canine friends.

I'm grateful to my college pals Burt Levinson and Joel Rosenfeld, who enjoy and foster my writing endeavors primarily because they fear that I will write a telltale book about our days on- and off-campus.

I will always be grateful to the celebrated cartoon character "Inspector Gadget" who had the good sense to introduce me to one of my oldest friends and supporters, Andy Heyward.

My appreciation goes to Mindy Gross and Andre Orban for their friendship and their fanatical support of my phobic revelations, although my disclosures frequently scare them to death.

A nod to a class act, John Butterfield, my haberdasher, for his talent for insuring that I look stylish and for his words of praise for my writing.

124

I would also like to thank Christopher Caines, who demonstrated great skill in organizing my writing, correcting my spelling, making sense out of my third-grade grammar, and bringing it all together into a cohesive package. Christopher clearly related to the subject matter, which in itself is a scary thought.

My gratitude goes out to Elliot Kreloff for coming up with an imaginative and whimsical cover design consistent with the theme of the book. He clearly has an affinity for the mindset of phobics.

Finally, I want to thank my daughter, Susan, my son-in-law, Jeffrey, and the grandchildren, Jason and Andrew, for always believing in me. They are an amazing bunch, and like me they are all afraid to step on the cracks in the pavement for fear that something terrible will happen . . . and it will.

I am grateful to all of you, discerning readers, and I leave you with one final thought. In the words of Woody Allen, "I am thankful for laughter, except when milk comes out of my nose."

## ABOUT THE AUTHOR

Roger Lefkon has spent more than four decades in the entertainment industry earning a reputation as an accomplished producer, writer, director and television executive. He has also appeared at Madison Square Garden as a guest clown with the Ringling Bros. & Barnum Bailey circus and has been diagnosed by leading medical experts, specializing in human behavior, as being a world class phobic.

Always looking for diversions from his demanding schedule he has tried his hand at big wave surfing, tap dancing, rock climbing, discovering new sexual positions, bungee jumping, training parrots to speak Hebrew, Karate and Alligator wresting and has failed miserably at each endeavor although he did give an aging gator a run for his money before succumbing.

A transplanted New Yorker, the author and his lifetime partner and confidant, Phyllis Klein, reside in Beverly Hills, California. She would like nothing better than to retire from her PR business but is fearful of doing so since it would mean hanging out with him and his ever expanding collection of phobias 24/7.

Made in the USA
Lexington, KY
10 July 2013